ISBN 0-7673-9080-6

Dewey Decimal Classification
Number: 248.83

ject Heading: Youth—Religious
e. Bible—Study and Teaching

e believe the Bible has God for its
thor, salvation for its end, and truth,
ithout any mixture of error, for its
tter and that all Scripture is totally
true and trustworthy. The 2000
statement of *The Baptist Faith and
Message* is our doctrinal guideline.

nless indicated otherwise, Scripture
otations are from the Holy Bible,
ew International Version, copyright
3, 1978, 1984, by International Bible
Society.
Used by Permission.
ted in the United States of America.

for
Life
After
High
School

LIFEWAY PRESS
Nashville, Tennessee

Contents

Foreword

by Richard Ross

Imagine you were about to take your first bungee jump. We're not talking about the little bungee jumps at an amusement park, but one from a high bridge over a gaping canyon. Also suppose the equipment expert who is helping you get rigged up is called away and another equipment person is called in to finish up. Looking down to the canyon floor below, how important would it be to you that the two workers had covered all the bases with your gear? How important would it be that the second guy completely finished what the first guy started?

While we are asking obvious questions, here is one more. What are the odds you would have ignored the help of the second guy and just jumped off the bridge with your rigging half finished?

Without doubt, leaving adolescence for young adulthood is a bungee jump. Some make the jump fine. Some crash on the ground below. In our analogy, the first equipment expert represents caring and competent youth leaders in your high school church. They have been doing all they can to prepare you for life. However, they always run out of time before they finish the job. They leave you standing on the bridge with your rigging incomplete.

The second equipment expert represents caring and competent ministry leaders in the church where you will be a part of a college or young adult ministry. They have brief years to cooperate with God in finishing your preparation.

Being active in church during high school but avoiding church in young adulthood guarantees that some of your jumping gear will be unfinished. A disaster could result.

After you leave home, there will probably be no one will awake you on Sunday mornings, nor will anyone particularly care whether you attend church or not. You simply must decide on your own that one way you will reflect the lordship of Christ is through a commitment to a local church. Your jump to adulthood will be much less dangerous.

You probably have a personal relationship with Jesus Christ. Because of that, you likely will want to live for Christ as an adult. The Bible studies and pages that follow will help you think carefully about your transition from high school to young adulthood. At least six areas of life are addressed in the special features and Bible study experiences.

1. Spiritual Life and Gifts. To this point in life, others primarily have served you. Now you almost are ready to stand on your own two feet and make your own kingdom impact. The discovery of your unique constellation of spiritual gifts and God's plan for your life should give you confidence that you have all you need to handle life and to fulfill the purpose for which God created you.

2. Heritage. These days you are spending much more time thinking about the future than the past. That is as it should be. Even so, you are wise to spend a few moments thinking about the chapter of life you are now ending.

Like the space shuttle, your internal engines are about ready to place you in final orbit. That's a pretty neat trick. Just remember, though, that the shuttle's internal propellant and engines could never have gotten it into space. The liquid and solid fuel boosters are absolutely essential to break away from the Earth's gravitational pull. It is only after they have done their work and have fallen away that the final navigation to orbit can begin.

If you grew up in the church, a small army of nursery workers, grade school leaders, and youth workers have been your boosters for almost two decades. This book will help you value the incredible investment they have made in your future.

3. Commitments and Relationships. I belong to the generation of the early '70s that waved signs and marched in the streets. Though our causes were sometimes ill conceived, we did believe in uniting our hearts and our voices to make an impact on the world.

Students on either side of the millennial shift are again uniting hearts and voices. This time committed Christian students are embracing a promise to God called the CrossSeekers Covenant. You may choose to link arms with your brothers and sisters in this growing movement.

4. Looking Ahead. For years you have been surrounded with people responsible for showing you what is right and what is wrong. In the months ahead you will see fewer and fewer of those folks around. More and more it will be up to you to make the hard decisions. Though some issues are black and white, many more are varying shades of gray. You need the specific guidance in the following pages to help you make the hard calls.

5. Ministry and Missions. As you may know, the Dead Sea in the Middle East is devoid of life because water flows in but never flows out. A life that receives but never gives is equally stagnant.

It is now time for you to discover ways for you to allow all that has flowed into you for 18 years to flow out to others. It is time for you to find ministries that allow you to be a servant.

It is likely God will call you to serve in a missions setting in the next few years. God is calling out thousands of young adults to give a semester, summer, or year in missions service. If you join this rising army, your life will never be the same.

6. Stewardship. Every young adult needs the life skill of effective money management. For the Christian, this is doubly true. Christian money management becomes a way to ensure life priorities are in order. It also becomes another tool for making a kingdom impact. Stewardship also involves the way we manage our time and resources. It is a subject that deserves careful attention.

A growing number of Christian leaders believe that students may be the generation through whom God plans to bring a fresh revival to the church. If revival breaks out in many places and if revival spills out of the church and begins to affect the fabric of society, it is possible a true spiritual awakening could emerge.

It is a mistake to put God in a box—to say He will bring revival in the next few months or years and that He will place students at the forefront of that revival. Sovereign God can do exactly what He pleases. But you can't help wondering.

If you are part of the revival generation, your transition from adolescence to young adulthood is even more crucial. You can't afford to walk far from God or you could miss the whole thing. On the other hand, if you acknowledge Him in all your ways, He will direct your paths—including a possible path toward revival.

The youth leaders in your present church care about you. They have invested scores of hours in you, and they care about your transition to young adulthood. That is why they have placed this book in your hands. In a sense, they will be your cheering section in the months and years ahead. If you take the steps of growth described in the following pages, they will have plenty to cheer about.

Richard Ross is the youth ministry consultant in the Pastor/Staff Leadership Department of LifeWay Christian Resources of the Southern Baptist Convention.

A Fresh Start

In the Beginning . . .

Have you ever wished for a fresh start? You are not alone. God Himself is the originator of fresh starts.

He made a fresh start in creation. In a blast of creative activity, God spoke into being a universe bursting with energy. Galaxies of stars and planets flung out from His creative spark. On a small planet in a small galaxy, God created one additional wonder—humans!

His creative process continues. He made a fresh start when you and I were born. Our entry into the world forever changed the history of the universe. Your birth alone changes all the equations and dynamics of history.

Startling? You bet.

Your new birth in Christ is definitely a new start. When you experience Jesus Christ in salvation, you make a new beginning. In that new relationship alone, you have the power to live a changed life.

You also experience new starts at special times in life; like when you graduate from high school. It's like a new beginning. A fresh start.

What will your fresh start be like? What kind of person do you want to be? Let's check up to see if we are on the right track. Think about and list some of the essentials for your new start after high school. What would be your five top priorities for a fresh start?

Scripture Passages:
Genesis 1:26-27;
Psalm 8;
Colossians 3:1-10
Lesson Truth: God made you in His image.
Lesson Aim: To recognize God's image in yourself by:
• acknowledging God's desire for you to live a life pleasing to Him.
• identifying areas of compromise in your life and allowing God to change you.

My priorities for a new start:

1.

2.

3.

4.

5.

The Next Step . . . As you think about your priorities, it might be helpful to consider the kind of person you want to be. Ask yourself: Who am I? What kind of person am I becoming? What kind of person was I created to be?

Consider this: Locked within you is God's creative imprint. From the very beginning your unique personhood was a part of God's special gift to you. You are not the product of your parents, although you have been influenced by them. You are not the product of your peers, although you also are being influenced by them. There is a uniqueness about you that transcends all those influences. It is God-given. It harbors unusual energy and creativity. Because of God, there is nothing ordinary about who you are.

Well, you say, it sure doesn't look that way to me.

You are right, of course. How it "looks" to you rests on what you believe about God's work in creating you for just this time in the universe's history. Incidentally, your creation carries potential for good or for bad. Part of the mystery of creation is that it resides on the edge of chaos. God's

risk in giving His creation such potential is that it can be, and often is, used for great harm. Yet, greater still, is the potential for great good.

Below each, draw, list, or describe how you are like:

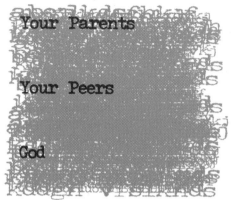

Your Parents

Your Peers

God

We will explore three Scripture passages to discover what issues meet us at our leap into fresh starts.

The Creator of Each of Us . . . In the book of beginnings, Genesis, we quickly discover an important truth. Read Genesis 1:26-27. God's image was planted into our being, like the DNA of each of our cells. Sin has altered that DNA causing aberrations of God's intended purposes. In salvation, we are given new life, growing from a new spiritual DNA that transforms our lives and our potentials.

In your opinion, how is sin like an altered gene in one's spiritual DNA?

In making a fresh start, it helps to rediscover the creative connection you have with God. You are part of His creative purpose. He placed great value on you from the beginning. Like a work of art, God spared no beauty in bringing you into being. You became like a mirror reflecting His image.

Sometimes, we take potshots at ourselves. We feel ugly, or worthless, or flawed. We belittle ourselves as insignificant or inadequate. We forget who created us. We listen to the voices of those who belittle God and His creation. Sometimes the voice is our own. Sometimes it is the voice of the people around us—like our families, or even those who don't seem to like us.

God's image is in the spiritual dimension—a capacity for spiritual understandings and living. The spiritual dimension goes beyond the mere physical. We are more than just bodies. Our bodies connect us with the physical universe. Our spirits connect us with God's spiritual universe. In real time that means we do nothing that does not touch our spirit.

If your best friend said to you there is no such thing as a "spiritual dimension," what would you say to him or her?

So Who and What Are We? . . . Here we turn to Psalm 8 for insight. Imagine a dark night out under the sky. White dots speckle the sky and if you get away from the lights of a city and the sky is clear, you can begin to see just how many stars there are. Or download pictures from the Hubble telescope on the Internet. Those pictures capture the dynamics

Like a work of art, God spared no beauty in bringing you into being.

still going on in the universe. You can see the residue of exploded stars like huge rings of dust and debris spiraling outward. The universe is immense. The writer of Psalm 8 did not have a Hubble telescope, but he did have a clear night sky. He understood the immenseness of God's creation. Stacked alongside the universe, it seemed to him man was insignificant.

Yet, he knew that was not the full story. He saw God's majesty in creation. The God he knew and served was no insignificant being. His creative work was spectacular and huge. Ever wonder why God created so much? Ever wonder what such a big creation has to do with you?

The psalmist's question is a good one. It applies to us in making a fresh start. Who are we? What is mankind? Why should such an awesome Creator pay the least bit of attention to a speck of cosmic dust like us?

How does being "cosmic dust" make one both insignificant and highly significant at the same time? Explain your answer.

The beginnings of an answer to that question lie in the fact that God created that speck of cosmic dust—that thinks and wills itself—in His image. In the least amount of "stuff" God has imbedded the essence of spiritual capacity. So while galaxies go cascading around the universe crashing into and gobbling up each other, and our own eases on to whatever destiny awaits it, we have a unique destiny with the Creator. We have creative work to do and a creative will to explore.

So let's get our bearings.

1. God is our Creator.
2. We aren't very significant compared to some things—like universes, and angels.
3. We are part cosmic dust, that is, we are made of the stuff of the universe.

In the last century, Darwin tried to explain us as the result of natural selection processes blindly at work. Today's scientists are at least beginning to recognize a purposeful process at work. Marx tried to explain us as mere economic tools. Freud tried to explain us as a bundle of sexual drives. At least they were trying to understand. We do have to acknowledge our connection with animals, with economies, and with sexual drives—they are part of our created reality. Yet, there is much more than that. There is something Godlike in all of us!

4. We are cared for by God and are given a stewardship of will.

We rule over much of the created order. We have been given great liberty when it comes to choosing what we will think and do. We are not just biologically driven. We have choices. We are constantly altering our course through life.

OK. Sounds really weird. Take a few minutes and check out what Psalm 8:1-2 says. The miracle of birth, the cries and laughter of children are praise to God. The laughter of a child exceeds the praise of a "Hallelujah Chorus."

Check out point 2 and 3 above and then read Psalm 8:3-5. Not quite God, but more than animals.

Check out point 4 above and read Psalm 8:6-7.

Now take these elements of your life, and number them in the order of their importance making a fresh start to fulfilling God's creative purposes in you.

Job
My will
Making choices
Sexual drive
Creativity
My past
My future
How I treat people
How I treat animals
How I treat things
My spiritual being

Which road will you take?

A fresh start begins with critical choices. Which road will you take? You are sitting at the intersection of high school and life beyond high school. Routines will change. Controls will shift. Your choices will expand. The impact of what you do will increase. You will choose the paths of your life as never before. And like a skier on a sharp downhill slope, what lies over the crest or the next drop may give you the thrill of your life or it may mangle you beyond recognition. This is no time to think it doesn't make any difference what you do to your own life.

Paul recognized this fact when he wrote a letter to some early Christians. Read Colossians 3:1-4.

Here, again, we need to nail down a truth. We cannot change ourselves by making new rules to follow. Rules cannot change lives. Only a spiritual transformation in Christ will change a person's life. Nothing else works. It was only because the Colossian Christians had been raised with Christ

that they could consider making new choices for living. People cannot transform themselves. The changes take place from within. Our choice to live a higher kind of life must come from a transforming experience with Christ. Once transformed, we can then set our sights on higher goals.

So, before you start setting rules, check your relationship with Christ. Is Jesus a reality in your life? Do you desire to follow Him and do things the way He would do them were He in your shoes? He knows all about what you are facing, so there's nothing about your situation that surprises Him. He loves you just as you are, but is ready to transform you into what you are capable of becoming through Him. He knows the "old" you is dead. He's ready to launch you on a new journey of discovery bringing the "new" you into being. And He makes that journey with you.

How would you describe how Jesus has transformed your life when you experienced faith in Him? Have you had such an experience? If not, ask a trusted Christian friend to tell you how to experience salvation—the most important fresh start one ever makes.

There are some things that need to be put to death as we make our fresh start on the high road. Paul listed five things that relate to our earthly nature. Such things as sexual immorality, impurity, lust, evil desires, and greed. These should not surprise us as unfitting for the Christian way. Yet, we struggle with them. It is precisely because they relate to our basic nature that we struggle. We look to satisfy appetites of sex and pleasure apart from moral concerns, control of others for our needs and desires, and control of money and power to enhance our selfish wants. The issue then becomes one of self-centeredness, whatever its expression. Sexual sins and greed are expressions of a carnal nature. It is the animal-like passions that control and dominate a spiritual being.

How many of Paul's list do you currently struggle to overcome? Are you willing to let Jesus Christ help you overcome them?

The second list of five sins emphasize wrong attitudes and wrong relationships with others. From Paul's vantage point, "anger, rage, malice, slander, and filthy language" (abusive language) were just as much sins of the flesh as sexual immorality. Some Christians think when they refrain from sexual sins, they become free and clear of sin. Yet, when they express hatred, malice, and use abusive language toward those engaged in such sins, they only indicate how much they are still

What does the "new me" look like?

caught up in their own sinfulness.

How many of Paul's list of attitudinal and relational sins do you struggle with? Are you willing to let Jesus Christ help you overcome these as well?

Before their conversion, the Colossian Christians had walked in all the sins Paul described. The sins determined their behavior. Now, they had been transformed. It was to be the new life in Christ that determined their behavior. For some, it took a while to work out. We find ourselves "being transformed." If you are struggling with sins of a sexual nature, or sins of attitude, take hope. In Christ, there is transformation. He does not reject you. Instead, He patiently and lovingly draws you toward the new you.

How do we know this? Paul would

not have written such a letter unless he knew Christians were in a process of becoming more like Christ. So keep focused on the higher road. Remember, Jesus walks beside you at every step.

Describe how knowing that Jesus will walk with you every step in the process of becoming like Him will help you to overcome your sins.

Paul wrote "the new self, which is being renewed in knowledge in the image of its Creator" (Col. 3:10). This is evidence of a process at work. The transformation has begun. It continues as we gain new knowledge and understanding of the Creator's image within us.

You and I are being remade in His image. What does the "new me" look like? The more we grow, the more we begin to look like Jesus—not physically—after all no one living really knows what Jesus looked like. We become like Him in willingness to follow God's will, in being loving, in being down-to-earth or real, yet focused on beyond-the-earth life. In short, you and I are living out Christ's mission upon the earth.

What are you now doing that doesn't fit being a "new" person in Christ? What do you want to ask

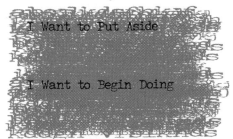

I Want to Put Aside

I Want to Begin Doing

God to help you put aside and replace with a new behavior?

Make a Fresh Start! A fresh start. Here's how you do it.

First, check your gear: 1. I'm created in God's image. 2. I know who I am. 3. I chose the high road. 4. I can't do it myself, I am letting Christ do it in me. 5. It's a process. Gear checked.

Second, set your sights. Above. Where God is. Reaching out of the earth and beyond the stars.

Third, go! It's time to let go. Just do it. Take the leap of faith. Don't look back. You are set on a new course. Go for it. Your time has come!

Keith Wilkinson, the state Sunday School director for Oklahoma, is the writer of this lesson.

EXTRA CREDIT

1. Based on a fresh start you would like to make, write a personal mission statement.
2. Memorize Colossians 3:8-10.
3. List two strengths and two weaknesses in your life. Then, list some possible ways to eliminate the weaknesses and build on the strengths.
4. Write down five goals you would like to accomplish before your 25th birthday.
5. Read the feature, "Remember Where You've Been on pages 12-14.

Remember Where You've Been

by Deanna Harrison

They were ready to put their pasts behind them and move on.

A hush fell over the crowd as the keynote speaker began his address. Many of those gathered could hardly believe "The Day" had finally arrived. It had been so long in coming. So many years of hard work and study. So much to learn and remember! The research and exams seemed endless. At times the people had become weary and discouraged. Some even wondered if they would ever make it. Their misgivings were well-founded since, tragically, some did not.

But "The Day" had finally arrived and the years of hard work were going to pay off after all. Throughout the years the students had grown and developed in ways they had never imagined. They had learned how to live and how to make wise decisions—if, of course, they chose to do so. They had learned how to treat one another and how to respond to authority. They had learned, some through firsthand experience, that their actions always have consequences. Their years of learning had been a time of incredible growth—a time when they learned about doubt and faith, fear and trust.

And now they actually stood on the threshold of their future. A future filled with hopes and dreams—a future faced with excitement and anticipation. They were ready to put their pasts behind them and move on.

But putting their pasts behind them wasn't what they needed. As they took their first steps into the future, what they needed most was to remember where they'd been. Listen to portions of the speaker's address as he challenged his audience to use their past as the foundation for their future:

"Remember how the LORD your God led you all the way . . . to humble you and to test you in order to know what was in your heart, whether or not you would keep his commands. . . . Know then in your heart that as a man disciplines his son, so the LORD your God disciplines you. . . . Be careful that you do not forget the LORD your God, failing to observe his commands, his laws and his decrees. . . . then your

heart will become proud and you will forget the LORD your God. . . . You may say to yourself, "My power and the strength of my hands have produced this wealth for me." But remember the LORD your God, for it is he who gives you the ability to produce. . ." (Deut. 8:2,5,11,14,17,18).

The time had come for the children of Israel to graduate from the school of the wilderness and move on to a higher level of learning awaiting them in the promised land. Moses knew, however, that the key to the future lay in remembering the past. He encouraged his people to remember where they had been. It seemed they had faced every difficulty imaginable. Yet through it all, God had been with them to teach, guide, and protect.

What obstacles have you faced in the past four years? How has God helped you overcome them? How can that knowledge of your past positively influence your future?

Moses reminded his audience that God disciplined them because they were His children. Solomon said it this way: *My son, do not despise the LORD'S discipline and do not resent his rebuke, because the LORD disciplines those he loves, as a father the son he delights in* (Prov. 3:11-12). Divine discipline is clear proof God is present and active in the lives of His children. And God's presence is proof of His love.

How has God disciplined you as you've grown spiritually? What difference has it made in your life? Do you have a better understanding of God's love because of His discipline?

Moses encouraged the people to remember God's words because those words would guide them through an uncertain future. Earlier in his "commencement address" Moses had instructed his audience to put God's

word at the heart of their conversation. *Impress them on your children. Talk about them when you sit at home and when you walk along the road, when you lie down and when you get up* (Deut. 6:7).

Moses knew that circumstances would change. Political and spiritual leaders would change. Family and friends would change. But God would never change (Mal. 3:6). The prophet Isaiah put it this way: *The grass withers and the flowers fall, but the word of our God stands forever* (Isa. 40:8).

As a graduating senior you will face some, if not a great deal of, uncertainty. Will all of your plans materialize? If not, what then? In times of uncertainty, you can draw upon God's Word for strength and guidance. What specific verses have guided you in the past? Write the references in the space below. Better yet, put them in prominent places (mirror, dresser, car) to remind you of them daily. Refer to them often for wisdom and encouragement.

Moses challenged the people not only to remember God's words but to obey them. Imagine driving down a highway and ignoring road signs indicating Stop or Wrong Way. What good are warnings and instructions unless they are obeyed?

Regular study of God's Word helps keep things in perspective. As you look toward the future, continually look back to God's Word and be reminded of what it says about such topics as time, rest, peace, money, friends, integrity, righteousness, purity, and holiness. If you're not sure about an issue, search the Scriptures. Concerning God's Word, *You will do well to pay attention to it, as to a light shining in a dark place* (2 Pet. 1:19). God's Word shines light on your world. Read it, obey it, and allow it to change your life.

Moses also challenged the people to remember that their ability to be successful came from God. Their future was bright and filled with hope. With God they would experience incredible victories. Without Him or His power and direction, however, they would fail miserably.

What things have you accomplished over the past four years? Write a description of the honors and awards you've received in the space below.

What did you do to accomplish such things? What part did God play? Have you given Him credit? Do you believe God wants to be involved in your future successes? How does that affect your relationship with Him?

One of the greatest gifts God gave the children of Israel was leaders such as Moses and Joshua. When they were fearful and full of doubt, Moses led them through the wilderness (Ex. 16). When they were disobedient to God, Moses interceded on their behalf (Ex. 32:30-32). When God's direction for their lives made no sense at all, Joshua faithfully led them to victory (Josh. 6).

What spiritual leaders has God placed in your life? List them below.

Consider these categories as you make your list: parent(s), siblings, ministers, youth workers, coaches, school teachers, boss, older youth, relatives, friends, friends' parents. How have each of these people influenced your life? How are you different because of knowing them? Over the next few weeks, make it a point to let each one of them know of the impact they've made on your life.

When Moses delivered his address to the children of Israel, he reminded them of specific events, spiritual milestones so to speak, that had occurred throughout their journey. Events such as the time God provided food when they had none, and another time when He provided water from a rock in the parched desert. And of course there was the event that started their whole journey—God's deliverance from Egypt where they had been slaves. The memory of each event would give strength and courage for whatever lay ahead. Remembering their past would have a profound impact on their future.

What events of the past four years do you consider to be spiritual milestones? (camps, retreats, mission trips, revivals, conferences, etc.) How did these events affect your spiritual growth? How can the memory of them affect your future? Take a moment right now and thank God for giving you these spiritual milestones to prepare you for an exciting and fulfilling future. Then remember them.

Deanna Harrison, a pastor's wife from Topeka, KS and experienced young adult and youth curriculum writer, wrote this feature.

One on One

How can my life have real meaning on a daily basis?

Be Like Mike. . . Growing up as an army brat, Michael moved 15 times in his first 18 years of life and attended nine schools. Mobility became a way of life. Adjusting to new environments and developing new relationships was expected with each move. Since change was so much a part of his life, he clung to the two things that remained consistent: his family and his relationship with Jesus Christ.

As his father was transferred from state to state, the family quickly settled in a new house and found a church home. Michael searched for a common thread that would enable him to weave himself into each new school. He became very interested in sports, especially wrestling, a sport in which he excelled. As a senior he held a 33-1-1 record. He was heavily recruited and signed with Colorado State University.

Now as graduation nears, change once again will define his life. He is going to leave all that is familiar: family, friends, coaches, his church, and school. The time has come to branch out. Michael knows he is not alone. The consistency of Christ is abiding in his life.

As you find yourself facing change in your life, are you remaining in Christ? All God asks is that you be willing to do what He wants you to do. The way you know what He desires of your life is to remain (abide) in Him. To abide means *an unbroken connection on a daily basis.*

Scripture Passages: Psalm 5:1-3; 95:1-7; John 15:4-11

Lesson Truth: Consistent personal worship is essential in order to have daily significance.

Lesson Aim: To practice personal worship in your life by:
- identifying reasons for personal worship.
- developing a plan to establish a habit of consistent time alone with God.

15

Remain in Christ. . . Take

a few minutes and read what Jesus said about abiding in John 15:4-5.

Jesus shared with His disciples an allegory of the vine, the vinedresser, and the branches in these verses. God is the vinedresser. He has the responsibility of cultivating the soil and protecting the vine. He is responsible for the drastic pruning of the branches and the cutting off of the bad ones. This is an ongoing process. It is through this care that the vineyard produces the best fruit. Jesus identified Himself as the true vine. He is strong and is supported by the constant and intensive care of the vinedresser. The branches represent Christians. They are dependent on the vine for life. Vines provide the root system, the nourishment, and the strength for growing and ripening the fruit on the branch. It is through the vine, *Jesus Christ,* that the branches, *Christians,* receive spiritual food for daily living.

How can you cultivate that daily relationship?

Select a quiet place.—This needs to be a place you can be alone without distractions (Matt. 6:6). Set aside time each and every day. God wants to spend time with you daily (Mark 1:35).

Secure your supplies.—You need a Bible, pen or pencil, a journal or notebook, and a devotional piece.

Settle on a plan of action.—
• *Pray.*—Prayer is our approach to God. You are preparing to enter His presence.
• *Read.*—Read the Scripture passage from the Bible. You may choose to read the Scripture listed in a daily devotion book or magazine like *essential connection,* you are using or a chapter from a book of the Bible.
• *Write.*—What has God said to you

through the reading of His Word? Are you really listening to Him? Write your thoughts in a journal or notebook.
• *Meditate/Write.*—Write a prayer in your journal or notebook that reflects your thinking concerning the passage you have just read.
• *Read.*—If you are using a devotional book, read the devotional reading.
• *Pray.*—Your prayer should ask God for opportunities to apply or live out what was gleaned in your daily Bible reading. This is also a time to voice prayers of adoration (praising God for who He is), confession, thanksgiving, intercession (praying on behalf of others), and petition (praying on your behalf).

As you spend time daily with God, expect Him to do something in your life only He can do.

In the space provided, write your response to these two questions.

How much time have you spent with God in prayer or in His Word this past week?

Would you say you have given high priority to your relationship with God?

The Difference

I got up early one morning and
rushed right in to the day;
I had so much to accomplish that I
didn't have time to pray.
Problems just tumbled about me, and
heavier came each task;
"Why doesn't God help me?" I
wondered.
He answered, "You didn't ask."

I wanted to see joy and beauty, but
the day toiled on gray and bleak;
I wondered why God didn't show me.
He said, "But you didn't seek."
I tried to come into God's presence;
I used all my keys at the lock.
God gently and lovingly chided.
"My child, you didn't knock."

I woke up early this morning and
paused before entering the day;
I had so much to accomplish that I
had to take time to pray.
Author Unknown

We live in such a fast-paced world that we give less and less time to God. This is the very time we need Him most. Read Psalm 46:10a.

The vinedresser knows that in order for a vine to produce its best crop, it must remain dormant during the winter months. God is not asking us to become dormant, but rather He is asking us to slow down and spend time with Him on a daily basis. He wants us to "be still and know" He is God.

Read Psalm 5:1-3. This Psalm is a morning prayer. The psalmist wanted to come before the Lord, one on one, in prayer each morning before he began his day. This day, David cried out to God concerning the difficulties he was experiencing with his enemies. He had confidence God would hear his prayer and answer.

Do you pray with expectancy? When you pray, you must:

• *Be yourself.*—Talk to God as if you were talking to your best friend. He wants to hear about your dreams, joys, hurts, sorrows, and requests.

• *Be consistent.*—We are to pray about everything. Read 1 Thessalonians 5:17.

• *Be expectant.*—Believe that God is

going to answer your prayers. Read Mark 11:24.

• *Be persistent.*—Keep on praying. Read Luke 18:1.

• *Be specific.*—How will you ever know if your prayers are being answered if your requests are voiced in general prayers?

Do you keep a prayer list? You can start one right now. For each day of the week, write the names of individuals for whom you will pray. Some may be mentioned every day. Then, write down special events, prayer concerns, and specific prayer requests that are personal to you. Beside each prayer request, write the date when you first added it to your list. As you begin to pray specifically, you are going to see God at work answering your prayers. Just as you wrote the date when you added the request to your list, be sure to write the date God answered. Remember, you learned you must be specific and persistent. In 1983, a prayer request was written down by two staff members on their own personal prayer lists. They began to pray for the salvation of one who served their church as a custodian. God provided opportunities for each one to share the plan of salvation, but the man never prayed to accept Christ. They

You want to be a strong, healthy branch who is producing a fruitful life.

continued to pray for him. All three individuals have moved from that church to various places in the United States, but they still stay in touch. Finally in September of 1997, the two staff members were able to write a date beside their answered prayer request. They had prayed 14 years for this man and in September he prayed to accept Jesus Christ as his Lord.

• *Be worshipful.*—You are entering the presence of God. Read Psalm 95:1-5. This Psalm, which begins with a hymn, is an invitation to worship God. Do you sing praises to God in prayer? God is worthy of our worship and our praise. He is to be adored. The psalmist exalts Him as "a great God" and as "our Maker." In verses 6-7, we are invited to *"Come, let us bow down in worship, let us kneel before the LORD our Maker; for he is our God and we are the people of his pasture, the flock under his care."* Your prayer time is a personal, one on one, time with your Heavenly Father. As you pray, you will want to voice prayers of confession, thanksgiving, intercession, and petition as well as praise.

Does your prayer list help you to stay directed? Prayer is a vital life line for our remaining in Christ.

Fellowship with Christ. . .
Read John 15:6. Just as the branch withers when cut off from the nourishment of the vine, we will wither when we are not in fellowship with Christ. Our lives become dry and empty. We become as useless to God as the dried up vines gardeners toss in the fire. Are you receiving the nourishment and life offered by Christ, the vine?

There is no better time to understand the importance of being in fellowship with Christ. Your life, like a branch, will be shaken in the next few months by the winds of change and the challenges ahead. The changes can be exciting, but they can also challenge you physically, emotionally, mentally, and spiritually. With these changes come competition for your time and energy, new voices to whom you will have to answer, new relationships, and new freedoms. The people who are familiar and have your best interest at heart will not be with you daily to cheer you on or sound the warning signals when things get out of alignment. Your life is sprouting in new directions. Are you in close enough fellowship with Christ that you can distinguish His voice? Begin now asking God to make you strong and courageous. Realize the pruning that may take place in your life is in order to cut away that which may keep you from being productive. You want to be a strong, healthy branch who is producing a fruitful life.

Stay Close to Christ. . .
Read John 15:7-8. In Luke 11:1 the disciples said to Jesus, "Lord teach us to pray." Think for a moment, if Jesus spent time daily with His Heavenly Father in prayer, how much more important is it for us to spend time talking and listening to God. The disciples saw the importance of prayer in Christ's example. This is the only recorded request the disciples made to Christ for instruction regarding spiritual disciplines. Although Christ taught many things, His disciples knew how urgent prayer would be for personal and spiritual growth.

As we remain in Christ, we experience a real need for prayer. The result of such abiding will be that a Christian will be able to ask anything in prayer and Christ will do it. A prayer from one abiding in Christ and from one whose heart is filled with

Christ's word will be a prayer from one who has intimate union and harmony with Him. Your prayers will be consistent with what God wants and will bring glory to Him. Read John 14:13-14, 15:16; 16:23.

In the space provided, write a paraphrase of these verses to help you have a clearer understanding of their meaning.

Abiding in Christ means that His teaching and His Word will permeate a Christian's lifestyle. As you were growing up, you probably heard on more than one occasion, "You look just like your mom," "You look just like your father," or "You can't mistake whose family you belong to." Your mannerism and your appearance were just two things that gave you an identity. When you look at your life, who do you see? Do you see yourself or Jesus Christ? Are you living a life that reflects your relationship with Christ? His character is to be reproduced in you and shared with others. That's what bearing fruit is all about. Read Galatians 5:22-23. Are these character traits found in the nature of Christ imitated in your life?

Abide in Christ's Love. . .
Read John 15:9-11. Jesus began this part of His discourse by pointing out that the model for His love toward the disciples was the Father's love for Him. His love for the disciples was pure, wholehearted, deeply personal, intelligent, enduring, and unconditional—just like the Father's. His commandment was to remain in this love. To remain in His

love, we will behave as He taught. Obedience would ensure the condition of abiding in His love. Obedience is a by-product of abiding in His love. Love expresses itself in acts of obedience. Jesus wanted them to abide in His love because He desired His joy to be in them.

Being a Christian equals being a joyous person. This does not come by chance but as an unexpected gift growing out of our intimate relationship with this One who is loved and served. It is joy that is an outward expression of an inward experience of God's grace. Real joy is nurtured and sustained when we experience spiritual growth.

Pamela Culbertson, youth minister at Royal Haven Baptist Church in Dallas, TX, is the writer of this lesson.

EXTRA CREDIT

1. Make a commitment to spend time alone with God for 21 consecutive days and then do it.
2. Memorize John 15:8.
3. Develop and maintain an updated, ongoing prayer list.
4. Set up an interview with someone whose spiritual maturity you respect, and talk to them about their methods for abiding in Christ.
5. Read a book on personal worship or prayer, and apply some of the principles you read about.

Where There's a Will, There's a Way

On Your Mark. . . Do you ever wonder if there is a grand design of the universe? I mean, look at all the stars and the galaxies and the solar systems. It is incredible when you think about it. At the same time, do you ever wonder if a God who is big enough to create all that would even remotely care about an individual person's life? Is there really a plan for your life you can follow? Another way to put it is this: Does God have a will for my life? If He does, what is it? Yes, He does!!

This study cannot possibly answer every question you may have about God's plan for your life, but it can help you set some guidelines on how to discover the plan and then how you can put it into practice.

Since you are doing this study you are either a senior who is about to embark on the rest of your life, or you have recently graduated and are making plans for collage, military service, a job, or even marriage.

As you begin, take a moment and list in the space provided a

Scripture Passages:
Deuteronomy 6:4-6
Romans 12:1-3;
Ephesians 5:17-20;
Lesson Truth: You can know God's will by submitting yourself to His control.
Lesson Aim: To discover God's will by:
• examining your relationship with God.
• surrendering yourself to God's leadership.

few of your dreams. Do you have some things in which you are interested or have you thought about what you want to do with the rest of your life? Write those down.

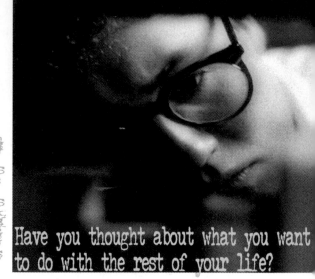

Have you thought about what you want to do with the rest of your life?

Get Set. . . As you contemplate your dreams and plans, it might be helpful for you to have a definition of God's will: It is His plan or purpose for our lives. That's pretty broad, but let's bring it down home a little by reading Romans 8:29, 1 Thessalonians 4:3-4, and 1 Peter 2:15.

We will take a look at some other passages later in the study that will help you know how you can put this will into practice, but essentially you get the picture of what God's will is:

• It is that you and I should become like His Son, Jesus.

• It is that we are to be "sanctified" or holy. The word, *holy*, means *to be set apart for God's use.*

• It is God's will that with our lives we would be an example of what He can do in a person's life.

What, then, does it mean to be like Jesus or holy? If you study the Scripture, you will find many qualities that characterize Christ, but here are a few for you for the sake of this study.

1. **Love.**—Jesus' character is one that is love. Read Romans 5:8. According to this passage, real love is accepting a person just as he or she is (while we were still sinners) and then offering one's self to meet the greatest need of

the person (Christ died for us). Christ demonstrated what real love is by His life. He is love. As Christians, part of our job is to have this characteristic of love in our lives.

2. **Service.**—Take a minute right now and glance through the first four books of the New Testament— Matthew, Mark, Luke, and John. Look at the headings of paragraphs. In the next few minutes, see how many times you can find where Jesus was serving someone or a group of people. You will discover Jesus was well known for His acts of service. His time here on earth was marked by ministry to others. Read Philippians 2:5-8 and you will find a description of that servant spirit. Again, we are to be servants just as Jesus was a servant.

3. **Others-centered.**—Jesus' main objective was to meet the needs of others. He did this without regard to His own needs. For further understanding of this read Philippians 2:3-4, where you will see how Paul encouraged the church at Philippi to think of others first.

4. **Honesty.**—Transparent is how Jesus was to those around Him, and when they looked at Him and spoke with Him people knew His life was

above reproach. He was always open and honest with those around Him. The New Testament is filled with examples of His honesty and transparency. Re-read the conversation between Nicodemus and Jesus in John 3 for an illustration of this.

5. Moral Integrity.—Jesus' life was morally pure. Read Hebrews 4:15.

So, Jesus was loving, serving, centered in other people, honest, and morally pure. As Christians, if we are going to be like Him then we will have those qualities in our lives as well. Here's the bad news: You can't do it. It is impossible for you to have these qualities in your life unless you have Him in your life. So here's the deal: You and I must allow Christ to live in our lives and control our lives so we can have His character.

The following story illustrates this point. It's called "Thirty Years and One Week," by Wes Seeliger (Published in *Faith at Work*, September, 1975). At the end of the story, write your reaction to it in the space provided.

He huffed and he puffed, but Peter Pan couldn't blow out all 30 candles on his birthday cake. At least not with one breath. For the first time in his life, Mr. Pan was frightened. *Thirty years old,* he thought . . . *I'm over the hill.*

That night he couldn't sleep. He tossed and turned . . . He got out of bed, went to the kitchen, turned on the light, and began writing. Although it was the middle of July, Peter Pan drew up a list of 80 New Year's resolutions. They would go into effect the first thing in the morning. His life would change.

No more parties. No cigarettes. No booze. Got to get a steady job. Must reduce. He would even cancel his subscription to *Playboy.*

He thought to himself, *All my life*
I've been too relaxed, too "hang loose." But all that will change. From now on I'm going to cut out the foolishness. It's time to get serious about life. Pan finished his resolutions at 3:00 a.m. But before turning in he set his alarm clock for 5:30. It was the first time in his life he had set the alarm.

Riiiiing! 5:30 a.m. Pan jumped out of bed. He was wide awake. "Thirty years and one day," he repeated to himself. He took the first cold shower in his life. He brushed his teeth up and down—like you're supposed to and marched out to live his first day of the "straight and narrow."

Monday—He burned his blue jeans and bought a gray suit.

Tuesday—He got a job in the bank.

Wednesday—He enrolled in a Dale Carnegie course.

Thursday—He took out a life insurance policy.

Friday—He subscribed to *Reader's Digest, The Wall Street Journal,* and *Time.*

Saturday—He began working out at the Mr. Executive Spa.

And then came Sunday. Peter Pan had hated church—at least in the old fun-time days. But now he was a new man. He still didn't like the idea, but he felt he must go to church. *After all,* he thought, *church is the ultimate in seriousness.*

Mustering all his willpower and determination, Pan put on his gray suit and marched to church. Once inside he knew he had made the right decision. It was quiet and dark. No talking. No foolishness.

Then the preacher climbed into the stately pulpit. He opened the large leather-covered Bible and began his sermon. Pan's chin dropped to the floor. He stared in disbelief as the preacher read the text for his sermon . . .

"Verily I say unto you, Except ye be converted, and become as little children, you shall not enter into the Kingdom of Heaven."

What is the main point of this story? Write your answer in the space below.

After you have responded to the story, think about this for a minute. It is God's will that you be like His Son. You cannot be like Him unless you accept Him into your life. You cannot accept Him into your life unless you ask Him to save you from your sins. Don't be guilty of what many your age are guilty. Don't get the cart before the horse. Many think that if they are good enough they can be God's child. So they do good things and act in a certain way, but you can't be God's child and you can't be like His Son unless you have Him in your heart and life. If you have not invited Christ to be the Savior of your life, please stop and do that right now. You will find a guide for doing so on the inside cover of this book. Unless and until you do this, the rest of the study will not make sense.

Once you have done this, you can proceed to the steps and guidelines that will help you to discover and put into practice God's plan for your life. Read Romans 12:1-3 to discover some guidelines to knowing and doing God's will for your life.

Here's how you can perform His plan for your life. These guidelines come straight from that Scripture.

1. Give yourself to God (v. 1).— The first 11 chapters of Romans give a description of what God has done for each of us. He has provided us with salvation from our sinfulness and provided a way for us to have a right relationship with Him. When the apostle Paul used the word, "therefore," he was asking the Roman Christians to reflect on all that God had done for them as he got ready to tell them (and us) what to do. To emphasize his point, Paul used the phrase, "in view of God's mercy," meaning that as Christians we do not get all that we deserve as sinners but what He wants to give us in Christ.

To offer our "bodies as living sacrifices" is to, by an act of our will, give all that we know and understand of ourselves to all that we know and understand of God. This decision is a conscious decision. Knowing God's will for us to be like His Son, we must deliberately choose for Him to be in control of our lives.

For a further understanding of what giving ourselves to God means, read Ephesians 5:17-20. Pay particular attention to verses 17 and 18. In the space provided, write a paraphrase of these verses

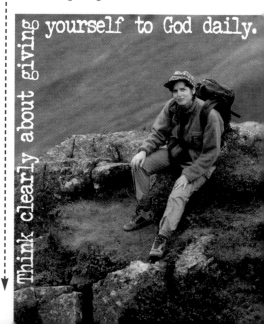

Think clearly about giving yourself to God daily.

to help you have a clearer understanding of their meaning.

In this passage, we can see what having Christ in control of our lives means. You probably know people who have had a little too much to drink. We use a phrase like, "he is under the control of the wine (beer or whiskey)." What that means is something other than the person is in charge of his or her life. For the Christian to give his or her life to God is to submit to the control of the Spirit (be filled with the Spirit) much like a person consciously chooses to be under the control of liquor. My intention is not to parallel being under the influence of alcohol with being under the control of the Holy Spirit, but I want us to see and understand that when we give ourselves to God we are voluntarily giving the control of every aspect of our lives over to Him.

This is not a one-time, never-to-be-repeated act. It is often done daily or even hourly. One man put it this way. I don't have any trouble being filled with the Spirit; it's just that I leak. This is not intended to imply that we can lose our salvation once we have made Christ a part of our lives. It does mean that we have to submit to His lordship on a daily basis. Think clearly about giving yourself to God daily.

2. Do not conform to the world's standards (v. 2).—One translation says, "Do not let the world squeeze you into its mold." Each of us is a unique person. Knowing and doing God's will can keep us from trying to be like everyone else. We shouldn't let our uniqueness get lost by doing, being, and thinking everything the way others do. Here's the catch on this. We cannot be like Jesus and like the world at the same time. The conscious decision to give ourselves to God will result in our not being like everyone else.

3. Let God transform you (v. 2).—The word, *transform,* is the Greek word from which we get our word, *metamorphosis.* Knowing and doing God's will is allowing God to gradually make us into a person who is like His Son. It is not a one time thing, but an ongoing result of the decisions we make to let Him control our lives. A caterpillar does not will itself to become a butterfly. It happens because it is the nature of metamorphosis. For a Christian to become like Christ, it is the natural result of Christ being in control of his or her life. It is a lifelong process, not an instantaneous happening.

This transformation takes place as we renew our minds. How can you do that?

Quickly, here are four steps:

• *Memorize Scripture.*—When you do, you will allow it to be flowing through your mind.

• *Feed your mind with healthy things.*—Here's an old computer saying, "garbage in, garbage out." You get the point, I'm sure.

• *Listen to the Spirit's inner witness.*—Because you are a Christian, the Holy Spirit lives within you. Be alert for impressions He gives you about what you ought to do and where you ought to go.

• *Act on what you know is right.*—Knowing and doing God's will can be a matter of doing what we already know to do. Read Scripture, pray, witness, be faithful to worship, be a faithful witness of what Christ is doing.

Think of some other things that you can do to renew your mind. List them here.

Read Deuteronomy 6:4-6. God has a plan for your life. Loving Him supremely will cause you to desire to do that will more than anything else in the world. It is not easy, nor is it a short-term commitment, but when you love Him you will want to please Him.

Here is one more practical thing about knowing and doing His will on a daily basis. I do not know anyone for whom God revealed His whole plan. It is a gradual revelation and understanding on the part of each individual. A word of advice that was given to me long ago about knowing and doing God's will is this: walk through the doors that are open. God has a plan for you. He wants you to know it. He will show it to you as you submit to Him. When He does, go through the open doors.

In the space below, list some doors that have already been opened to you and through which you have already walked.

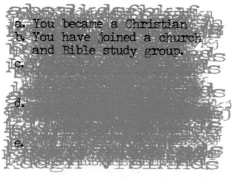

a. You became a Christian
b. You have joined a church and Bible study group.
c.

d.

e.

Go! If you have been around church for a long time, you probably have heard or read many of the things in this Bible study. In fact, you have probably been to camps or DiscipleNows or retreats that were based on these passages. So the question comes to you and me: Have we learned what they mean yet? Here's the truth: If we have not done them, we have not learned them. One person said it this way, "The final step in learning is application." So . . . go to it!

Chuck Gartman, lead youth Sunday School Consultant at LifeWay Christian Resources of the Southern Baptist Convention, is the writer of this lesson.

EXTRA CREDIT

1. Make a list of the areas in your life where you need to allow God to do some transformational work.
2. Memorize Romans 12:1-2.
3. Write a paragraph describing the plans you believe God has for your life right now.
4. On a separate sheet of paper, jot down the list of the five character traits of Jesus found on page 23. Jot down several ways you can demonstrate each character trait in your life now.
5. Interview a pastor or other church staff member to discover how he or she determined God's direction for his or her life.

A NEW TWIST TO
Spiritual Gifts

by Ann Cannon

Do you like quizzes with no right or wrong answers that tell you about yourself? Great! Here are two inventories that give you lots of cool stuff about YOU.

Learning Styles Uncovered

First, find out your learning style. Learning styles determine how you gather, sort, and remember information. Most people have one preferred learning style. To find yours, circle the number of the phrase that best completes each sentence. Stick with your first choice.

My favorite thing to do is to
1. visit with a friend.
2. read a book.
3. work on the computer.
4. daydream about my future.

My favorite TV programs are mostly
1. comedies.
2. news programs.
3. sports programs.
4. music videos.

My favorite type of class at school is
1. social studies, speech.
2. history, languages.
3. science, math, typing, physical education.
4. art, communications.

I enjoy learning when I can:
1. talk to others about their ideas.
2. gather information from books or experts.
3. use my hands to work on the problem.
4. be the first one to try something new.

When introduced to a new idea, I ask:
1. Why do I need to know this?
2. What do I need to know?
3. How does this idea work?
4. When can I try out the idea?

When working on a project, I would rather:
1. work with people.
2. work by myself.
3. complete the task as quickly as possible.
4. try several different ideas before settling on one.

I remember something better if I
1. can see and hear it happen.
2. research the facts.
3. can find a practical way to use it.
4. try it myself.

My least favorite way to study is by:
1. being quiet.
2. working with a group.
3. sitting still.
4. listening to a lecture.

My favorite way to do homework is
1. listening to music.
2. studying in silence.
3. building something.
4. looking at charts, maps, or pictures.

Others describe me as.
1. a sensitive, open person.
2. a smart person.
3. someone who gets things done.
4. uninhibited and fun.

Total the number of 1's, 2's, 3's, and 4's.
#1's____ #2's____ #3's____ #4's ____

If you have more 1's, you are a verbal learner, also called a feeler. If you have more 2's, you are a thinker. If you have more 3's, you are a doer. If you have more 4's you are a visual learner, also called an intuitor.

Feelers or verbal learners enjoy hearing others' stories and sharing their own experiences. These learners are sensitive to others' feelings. People with this learning style adapt well to new situations, enjoy being around others, like background music, and prefer to solve problems, especially in groups.

Thinkers are organized, practical, and prefer working from a plan. They quickly grasp the big picture, then look at the facts. Thinkers learn from the experts, rather than hearing others' opinions.

Doers learn by getting involved. They

like hands-on experience. Instructions and rules slow them down. Doers are energetic and depend on common sense.

Intuitors or visual learners are uninhibited, flexible, and willing to take risks. They creatively accept new challenges. Since they learn visually, they watch others and respond with sensitivity. They like variety with two or three major projects going at the same time.

Learning styles describe how you take in information or ideas. Let's look at what you can do with this information as a Christian youth.

Spiritually Gifted

God gave His first gift in the person of Jesus Christ. God's gift offered a way for all people to be saved. God provides additional gifts for believers in the church. Every Christian has at least one spiritual gift, and there are a variety of gifts in the same church. God gave these spiritual gifts to build up the church through ministries that will help others grow spiritually.

The Bible records several lists of spiritual gifts. Not all the spiritual gifts mentioned in the Bible are listed in the following inventory. There may be other spiritual gifts God has given you that aren't listed in the Bible. Ready to discover your spiritual gifts? OK, here's what you need to do:

1. Read each statement under "Discover Your Spiritual Gifts," recording your answer on the "Spiritual Gifts Inventory Score Sheet" under the related number.

2. Total each column on the score sheet, and write these totals at the bottom of the score sheet page. Those areas with the highest scores are your spiritual gifts. You may already recognize one or two of these; others may need to be cultivated.

3. To find out about your highest-scoring gifts, look under "Explanation of Gifts/How to Use Them."

Information In/Action Out

Is there a correlation between your learning style and your spiritual gifts? Perhaps God has given you spiritual gifts that complement how you learn so you feel comfortable in using your spiritual gifts. Here are a few ideas of how learning styles and spiritual gifts relate.

LEARNING STYLES

	Visual Learners/ Intuitors	Verbal Learners/ Feelers
	___ Mercy	Prophecy
	___ Hope	Evangelism
	___ Prayer	Encouraging ___
	Doers	Thinkers
	___ Sharing	Teaching ___
	___ Serving	Leadership ___
	___ Hospitality	Discernment ___

• The spiritual gifts of prophecy, evangelism, and encouraging require strong verbal skills, as well as sensitive people skills. The verbal learner may feel most comfortable with these gifts.

• The spiritual gifts of teaching, leading, and discernment involve skills in planning and organization. The Christian with these gifts needs to think clearly and know how to share that thinking in an easily-understood way. The thinker learning style may feel most comfortable with these gifts.

• The spiritual gifts of sharing, serving, and hospitality are practical, hands-on activities that appeal to the doer learning style. These spiritual gifts require lots of energy.

• The spiritual gifts of prayer, mercy, and hope complement the visual or intuitive learner. These gifts involve recognizing and responding to others' needs. This creative learning style complements the various way these spiritual gifts can be developed.

To find out if your spiritual gifts complement your learning styles, add together your scores for each spiritual gift listed in each quadrant of the learning styles circle. Does the quadrant with the highest total match your learning style? If so, look for ways your spiritual gift can help you learn. Look for ways your learning style can strengthen your spiritual gift. If your learning style and spiritual gifts don't match, remember you are a "work in progress"; God is not finished with you. Your learning style will change as you develop mentally and physically. Your spiritual gifts may change as you develop spiritually.

Explanation of Gifts/How to Use Them

Circle your top three spiritual gifts. Review the Scripture that supports these gifts. After each explanation of the gift are brief suggestions of how to put your spiritual gift to work. Begin looking for specific ways to use your spiritual gifts this week.

A. Prophecy (Rom. 12:6; 1 Cor. 12:10, 28; Eph. 4:11). Gifted in sharing God's truth powerfully and clearly; strong verbal skills; feels God's leadership in speaking out in personal conversation, as well as in larger groups; interested in politics, public concerns, and world issues, and how these affect God's people. *•preaching; •challenge others to live by God's standards*

B. Evangelism (Eph. 4:11). Gifted in sharing the gospel effectively with nonbelievers; feels great joy when someone accepts Jesus as Savior; relates personal testimony and introduction to Jesus in compelling way; is comfortable witnessing in any situation. *•witness regularly to those outside the church; •teach others to witness; •participate in churchwide visitation; •share testimony often*

C. Encouraging (Rom. 12:8). Gifted in speaking words of comfort, encouragement, or advice to help others do their best; sensitive to others' problems; provides revealing answers that others find helpful; confrontational, but not offensive; patient with others' weaknesses; willing to share past mistakes so others gain spiritual maturity. *•work in one-on-one ministry; •counsel others; •share testimony often*

D. Teaching (Rom. 12:7; 1 Cor. 12:28; Eph. 4:11; 1 Pet. 4:11, 5:1-2). Gifted in understanding and explaining the Bible to others; likes to research, analyze, and interpret facts; wants to guide others in understanding the Bible; willing to be an example for others; willing to learn as well as teach. *•share ideas in Sunday School; •teach younger children in VBS or other Bible studies; •lead a discipleship group for new Christians; •start a Bible study group at school*

E. Leadership/Administration (Rom. 12:8; 1 Cor. 12:28; 1 Pet. 4:10). Gifted in ability to see God's purpose, set goals, and lead others to reach that purpose; sees bigger picture; likes to plan, organize, and delegate; confident in standing before others; sees needs and gives leadership to meet needs; works hard; gives attention to detail. *•work with a committee; •choose a ministry that needs leadership; •form a new ministry where you see a need*

F. Discernment (1 Cor. 12:10). Gifted in evaluating whether an idea or situation comes from God, Satan, or humanity; has unique ability to distinguish truth from error; willing to warn others of the dangers of evil and confront wrong attitudes and actions. *•research false leaders and beliefs and share this information with others; •speak up against beliefs that water down Christianity*

G. Sharing/Giving (Rom. 12:8). Gifted in joyfully sharing material possessions; finds satisfaction when giving resources freely; sees financial needs that others overlook. *•motivate others to follow Christ's leadership in giving; •serve on a stewardship committee; •support mission emphasis; •give regularly to* *your church*

H. Serving/Helping (Rom. 12:7; 1 Cor. 12:28; 1 Pet. 4:10-11). Gifted in assisting those in leadership positions; sees everyday needs of people; likes to help in concrete ways; levelheaded in crisis situations; prefers to work behind-the-scenes to support and assist leaders. •*help in the nursery, the church office, or gym;* •*work on a low-profile committee;* •*offer to help decorate for an event, mail out regular newsletter, drive the church van*

I. Hospitality (1 Pet. 4:9). Gifted in helping others feel comfortable wherever you are; outgoing, informal, and friendly; likes to meet new people; willing to help without being asked; likes to fellowship with others. •*bring friends to youth activities;* •*greet visitors and stay with them during the session;* • *offer to show visitors around the church*

J. Mercy (Rom. 12:8). Gifted in immediate compassion and caring for those who suffer physically, emotionally, or spiritually; senses others' despair and pain; action-oriented; helps others share their feelings; finds happiness in doing deeds for those who don't deserve it. •*visit the ill in the hospital or those recovering at home;* •*offer to listen to others' problems; talk to those ignored by others*

K. Hope (Heb. 10:23,35). Gifted in seeing the best in people and events; sensitive to spiritual concerns; optimistic about others' motives and actions; not easily disappointed by others; bounces back quickly after being hurt; strong in difficult situations; patient in times of trouble. •*encourage friends to see hope;* •*share experiences where you found hope in time of difficulty;* •*point out the positive in a negative experience*

L. Prayer/Faith (1 Cor. 12:9; 14:15). Gifted in putting into words what the heart is saying; prays often and persistently; expresses affection and love in simple ways; willing to pray anywhere, any time; believes in the impossible; sees God's purpose in a situation and knows God will work it out.
•*pray in public;* •*stop to pray when someone mentions a prayer need;* •*be faithful in time alone with God*

Discover Your Spiritual Gifts

Use the "Spiritual Gifts Inventory Score Sheet" to record your answers to the following statements. Usually the first answer that comes to mind is the answer to record. There are no right or wrong responses.

1. I am not afraid to speak the truth.

2. I spend time with unbelievers so I can share my faith.

3. I usually can persuade people to do certain things.

4. I can make difficult Bible verses easier for others to understand.

5. Setting and achieving goals are

Spiritual Gifts Inventory Score Sheet

Write a number based on this description in the box under each statement's number.

This statement describes me	Score
I am never this way.	0
I am this way very infrequently.	1
I am this way some of the time.	2
I am this way most of the time.	3
I am this way all of the time.	4

1	2	3	4	5	6	7	8	9	10	11	12
13	14	15	16	17	18	19	20	21	22	23	24
25	26	27	28	29	30	31	32	33	34	35	36
37	38	39	40	41	42	43	44	45	46	47	48
49	50	51	52	53	54	55	56	57	58	59	60
A	B	C	D	E	F	G	H	I	J	K	L

To figure your score, total the numbers you wrote in each column. Write the total for that column under the letter at the bottom. Place a check mark by the three spiritual gifts for which you have the highest score.

A___ Prophecy	E___ Leadership	I___ Hospitality
B___ Evangelism	F___ Discernment	J___ Mercy
C___ Encouraging	G___ Sharing	K___ Hope
D___ Teaching	H___ Serving	L___ Prayer

important to me.

6. I notice sinful actions and attitudes before others do.

7. I like to help people without being asked.

8. It's not important that others know the good things I do.

9. I look for ways to meet new friends.

10. I find strength in helping others share their feelings.

11. I am not easily disappointed.

12. I am comfortable talking to God.

13. I will stand alone on something I believe in strongly.

14. I am drawn to unbelievers because I want to win them to Christ.

15. I give practical, step-by-step advice to those who come to me for help.

16. I enjoy studying the Bible and talking about it with others.

17. I like to organize, plan, and complete jobs given to me.

18. I feel compelled to make others face their sins.

19. I don't care who gets credit for a job well done.

20. I notice when others have a material or financial need.

21. I have the ability to make visitors feel comfortable.

22. I am attracted to those who are hurting.

23. I don't hold grudges.

24. Prayer gives me strength.

25. I feel an intense need to share God's love with others.

26. I enjoy participating in winning unbelievers to Christ.

27. I like helping others work out difficult problems in their lives.

28. I enjoy helping Christians understand key biblical truths.

29. Often others look to me for leadership.

30. I can recognize evil, even when it is presented as good.

31. I like projects that require a hands-on approach.

32. I often share my material possessions with others.

33. I like preparing food for others to enjoy.

34. I do kind deeds for people who cannot, or will not, return the favor.

35. I am an optimistic, positive person.

36. Because I believe in the power of prayer, others ask me to pray for them.

37. I feel God telling me to warn people that there will be divine judgment on sin.

38. I enjoy telling unbelievers about Christ's love for them.

39. Others call on me for advice when they are discouraged or confused.

40. I like to research, organize, and share information from the Bible.

41. If a group doesn't have a leader, I don't mind taking charge.

42. Others tell me that I have accurately warned them about the dangers of a false teaching.

43. I like helping others, but I don't expect anything in return.

44. I serve the Lord by giving financially to support Christian activities.

45. I like having others come to my home.

46. When I hear about someone who is lonely or neglected, I try to find a way to care for that person.

47. I believe all things eventually work out for the good.

48. I see God using difficult times to teach me to pray.

49. I am willing to speak out against sin and evil, even though I might be criticized or teased.

50. I have a deep burden to share my faith with people who do not know Jesus Christ.

51. I enjoy challenging others one-on-one to become all that God wants them to be.

52. I like working with a small group of Christians as they learn to grow spiritually.

53. I like coordinating the gifts and abilities of others as we work on a common task.

54. I can tell the difference in truth and error.

55. I would rather help people out behind the scenes, than minister in a more public way.

56. I give a tithe, and sometimes more, of my income to support God's work.

57. I try to make others feel welcomed and comfortable no matter where we are.

58. In a crisis situation I know what to do and say.

59. I am accepting of others' faults and failures.

60. I continue to trust God for what others think is impossible.

First Things First

Scripture Passages:
1 Samuel 15;
Matthew 6:25-33;
Luke 2:41-52

Lesson Truth: You can find balance in life by seeking God's kingdom first.

Lesson Aim: To lead you to find balance in your life by:
• identifying what is most important in life.
• developing your total person and by seeking God's kingdom first.

Decisions, Decisions! Life is all about choices, both large and small. Think about it; how many decisions have you had to make already today? When to get up, what to eat for breakfast, how to dress, whether to go to church, whom to sit by, whether to participate, and so on.

Some decisions are easy, such as don't do drugs or stay in school. But many choices aren't between good and bad. They are options between good, better, and best. So how do you make the best choices consistently?

It's fair to say you make choices based on what's important to you; in other words, according to your priorities. If making good grades is important to you, you probably spend a lot of your time studying. If a certain boyfriend or girlfriend is a priority right now, chances are you spend as much time as possible with him or her.

Ultimately, the seemingly insignificant daily decisions you make determine the direction of your life. So if you want to follow God's direction, you've got to make God's priorities your priorities.

Consider what your priorities are now. In the space below, list what you believe are your top five priorities. Write the five things, persons, or activities that are most important to you. As you proceed with this study, consider whether the five items you listed accurately

portray your priorities and whether any of them should be changed.

The Royal Who Messed Up Royally. . .

To discover what happens to people who have inappropriate priorities, read the story of King Saul in 1 Samuel 15. Saul was a guy who had everything going for him. He was the first king over Israel, chosen by God and anointed by God's prophet, Samuel. He was "an impressive young man without equal among the Israelites—a head taller than any of the others" (1 Sam. 9:2). He had also become a great military leader and hero among his people (1 Sam. 14:47-48).

Saul was riding high on this military winning streak when God gave him specific instructions through Samuel. Samuel told King Saul to attack and completely destroy the Amalekites. God's directions were explicit: no one was to be spared; every person and animal among the Amalekites was to be killed.

Why would God order the killing of defenseless women, children, and livestock? The Amalekites were guerrilla terrorists. They supported themselves by attacking other nations. They had attacked the Israelites when God's people first entered the promised land. They continued to raid their camps periodically. Israel could have no lasting peace as long as there were Amalekites. Also, the influence of the Amalekites was a threat to the Israelites' spiritual health. God did not want His people to adopt the idol worship the Amalekites practiced.

Saul followed Samuel's instructions, and attacked the Amalekites. He and his army triumphed over the enemy and destroyed them just as God had commanded—almost. Saul destroyed "everything that was despised and weak" (15:9), but he spared the Amalekites' king and the best of their livestock. When Samuel confronted Saul about his disobedience, Saul claimed his soldiers saved the animals to sacrifice to God.

God wanted total obedience from Saul. But Saul tried to substitute his own priorities—wealth for Israel and sacrifices for God. It was a huge mistake. Because of Saul's foolish decision, God rejected him as king. He lost God's favor, his kingdom, his popularity, and finally his sanity and his life because of his poor priorities.

Can you think of a time when you acted against God's priorities for your life and paid a price for it? What was the priority that governed your decision? What should have been the priority influencing that decision?

Don't Sweat the Small Stuff. . .

Let's say you don't want to screw up your life like Saul did. You really want to set your priorities according to God's standards and live in His will. But how do you determine what your priorities should be? What does God say should be most important in your life?

You'll find a great starting point for understanding God's priorities in Matthew 6:25-33. Read this passage and fill in the blanks below using the scrambled letters:

What do you think Jesus wants your top priority to be?

1. Jesus told His followers not to _____ (royrw) about what's not most important in life.

2. Specifically, He said not to be concerned about what you will _____ (tea) or _____ (nirkd) or _____ (arew).

3. He noted that God provides food for the _____ (dribs), and you are much more _____ (bellaauv) to Him than they.

4. Likewise, God _____ (stheolc) the _____ (sellii) of the _____ (delfi) in splendor. How much more He is willing to _____ (lochet) you!

5. Jesus taught His followers to make God's _____ (mokgdin) and His _____ (sthrunegioses) first priority.

6. If you do, Jesus said, all the things you need will be _____ (veing) to you.

Keep in mind that most of the people listening to Jesus didn't have large bank accounts. Some truly didn't know where their next meal was coming from or how they would be able to clothe their families. But you don't have to be poor to be overly concerned with having enough food and clothing. Sometimes those who have the most, worry the most about how to get more. That's why just prior to this teaching, Jesus had told His followers not to store up treasures on earth (Matt. 6:19).

Obviously, Jesus wasn't advocating laziness. He wasn't telling His audience to sit back and do nothing so God could pour riches into their laps.

Of course, God expects you to work for a living. But the key issue is priorities. God doesn't want you to let material things be the main focus.

When Jesus told the people not to worry about things like clothing and food, He was telling them not to let these concerns consume their thoughts. Examining your thought life is a good way to determine priorities.

What relationships, goals, or ambitions fill your thoughts? List a few answers as they come to mind. These may be clues to your priorities. Are they similar to the things you listed among your top five priorities on page 33?

Another tool for evaluating your priorities is the question: How do I spend my free time? and How do I spend my money? Again, answer these questions in the space below. Then consider: Is the way I spend my time and money consistent with what I say is most important to me?

In verse 32, Jesus said the pagans—those who don't know God—chase after material things. Those who belong to God are to be different. Are your priorities different from those promoted in the world?

Look through several popular magazines. Notice the ads and topics of articles. What things do these magazines suggest are important in our society? List as many as you can below.

Now consider: Are these priorities consistent with what God's Word says is important? Then ask yourself: Does my life give evidence of priorities in line with society's or God's Word?

In verse 33 Jesus spelled out exactly what God wants as your first priority. Above all else, He wants you to pursue His kingdom and His righteousness. But what does that mean?

The "kingdom of God" is the reign of God. All those who have trusted Jesus for salvation belong to God's kingdom. To seek God's kingdom is to desire to enter it, to bring others into it, and to submit to God's rule in one's life on a daily basis. To seek God's righteousness does not mean working to become righteous before God. We

Those who belong to God are to be different

can't earn a right standing with God. We can only receive that kind of righteousness as a free gift through trusting Christ for salvation. When Jesus told His followers to seek righteousness, He was challenging them to pursue God's will. Throughout His ministry, Jesus gave specific instructions for living in God's kingdom. To seek righteousness is to try to follow Jesus' teachings.

To put it another way, those who

living and neglect the more important things that don't scream quite as loudly for your attention. When that happens, you soon end up making choices that contradict your priorities. You say God is most important, but you don't find time to meet with Him. You say a friend is important, but you neglect him or her. Living out of sync with what you believe is important only leads to stress and frustration. So follow Jesus' example, and remember to keep first things first.

Jennifer Denning, experienced youth worker and youth curriculum writer from Alexandria, VA, is the writer of this lesson.

help me grow strong spiritually and physically? Am I devoting the necessary time to study but still making time for recreation and friendships?

In the space below, draw a pie graph that illustrates how you divide your time between: 1. academics; 2. spiritual disciplines (like Bible study, prayer, and worship); 3. physical fitness/exercise or athletics; and 4. friendships and family relationships. Is your life well balanced, or do you need to spend more time in one area and less in another?

Now that you have some guidelines for establishing priorities, you've got some work to do. It's easy to get busy with the urgent tasks of everyday

EXTRA CREDIT
1. Make a detailed list of priorities and post it in a prominent place for frequent review.
2. Memorize Matthew 6:33.
3. Make a list of some things you can do to give your life more balance spiritually, physically, socially, and mentally.
4. Do a biblical character study on Paul and determine his priorities.
5. Interview a person you respect about their priorities in life.

Stand Up and Be Counted

Are there any values by which I should live my life?

What Counts? Think about some of the prominent names of the twentieth century, names like Gandhi, Martin Luther King, Jr., Adolph Hitler, Mother Teresa, Billy Graham, and Al Capone. These were people who made a dramatic mark on the world because they held strong values (good or bad) that shaped the courses of their lives, and in the process impacted the world. Most people desire to make a difference, but don't really know how to make their lives count. These examples provide a strong clue. When you possess values that have the depth of convictions to shape your life, you will be able to make your own mark in the world.

But where do such strong values come from, and what kind of values should you seek? As the short list of prominent names above shows, strong values can be both positive and negative. You must be careful about what you choose to be the values that shape your life.

Can you name some influences that try to shape the values in your life? List them in the space below.

Scripture Passages: Daniel 3:1-30; Romans 6:1-23

Lesson Truth: God's values should affect your daily life.

Lesson Aim: To lead you to express why godly values should affect your daily life by:
• describing how the Scripture illustrates the difference godly values make in daily lives.
• determining what values should affect your daily decisions.

Perhaps you thought about influences you feel from your parents, your friends, your church, your school, advertisements, or popular entertainment. All of these, and more, constantly fight for your attention and compete for your commitment. At this stage of your life, you are gaining more and more independence. As you move from high school to higher education, the work force, the military, or even marriage, you will find you can no longer lean upon the values and convictions of others but must establish your own. The Bible has many examples of people who acted on strongly held values and convictions even in the face of severe opposition. Christians must, in turn, accept the challenge to adopt God's values as their own and shape the course of their lives with godly values.

The values y
hold not on
determine h
you live yo
life, th
determine h
you interpr
life in genera

Valuable Values. . . What are values? Look up *value* in a dictionary and write the definition(s) that seems to apply.

Now write your own definition of what a personal value is based on what you have read:

In a nutshell, your values are the principles, standards, character traits, or qualities you consider worthwhile, desirable, or right. The values you hold not only determine how you live your life, they determine how you interpret life in general.

List what you believe are your values in life:

In the opening chapters of the Book of Daniel, Babylon conquered the kingdom of Judah and took the most promising young men from Judah captive. The Babylonians hoped to assimilate these quality young men into Babylonian society and one day employ them in the service of the king. A regimented program of training and education was set up for these captives. Four of these captives are mentioned by name: Daniel (renamed Belteshazzar), Hananiah (renamed Shadrach), Mishael (renamed Meshach), and Azariah (renamed Abednego). Because of their strength of character, and the blessing of God upon them, these four young men found themselves in significant positions of leadership in Babylon within a very short time. Daniel 3:1-30 relates an experience of Shadrach, Meshach, and Abednego that reflects the values and convictions they held.

Read Daniel 3:1-7. Both Nebuchadnezzar and his subjects seemed to hold self-centered valued. He values his status and the adulation from others. The people valued their self-interests, which were served by giving the king what he wanted.

Read Daniel 3:8-12. A specific group appeared. This group was the well-established set of advisers/leaders in Nebuchadnezzar's kingdom. Although they probably claimed they were simply being patriotic and loyal to their king, most likely they were jealous of the rapid rise to prominence these three young men had experienced and protective of their own power. They valued their power and position and would do anything to preserve them.

Read Daniel 3:13-15. Talk about pressure! Nebuchadnezzar very much wanted these three men to share his own highest value—himself. Face to face with the furious king, and the blazing furnace already lit, Shadrach, Meshach, and Abednego were given the opportunity to save their lives. The easy thing would have been to give up their personal convictions and accept the king's values.

Earlier, you listed some sources that try to influence your values. What kind of pressures do you feel from those sources? Circle the pressures you experience:

Fear	Deception
A need to belong	Appeals to conscience
Guilt	Promise of pleasure
Promise of rewards	Love
Shame	Flattery
Appeals to image	Appeals to authority
Ridicule	Appeals to reason
Punishment	Other:

Although the pressures you face probably don't include death threats, many of these forces can be very powerful. If you are not prepared in advance to resist them, it is easy to be swayed by them.

Shadrach, Meshach, and Abednego were well prepared. Long before this incident, they had established some bedrock values and convictions. They didn't have to stop and think about how to respond. They knew! Look at their response in Daniel 3:16-18.

As young Jews, they learned at an early age the key Scripture of the Jewish people: "Hear, O Israel: The LORD our God, the LORD is one. Love the LORD your God with all your heart and with all your soul and with all your strength" (Deut. 6:4-5). They had learned the first and second commandments: "You shall have no

God doesn't promise to deliver you just because you make a stand for what is right.

Because this bedrock value was fully integrated into their characters, they were not influenced by their circumstances or threats. There was no question in their minds at all about bowing to this image of Nebuchadnezzar. It was not going to happen. Notice, too, just how deep their conviction ran. It didn't matter if they were thrown in the furnace—they were going to do what was right. It didn't matter if God delivered them— they were going to do what was right. As you read Daniel 3:19-30, you will discover in this case, God did choose to deliver them in a miraculous fashion. You will also discover that the strong value they had allowed to shape their lives in turn affected the course of history. Nebuchadnezzar changed his decrees and acknowledged the power of their God.

God doesn't promise to deliver you just because you make a stand for what is right. Although many folks in Scripture and history did find deliverance and protection, many others were martyred for their faith. Joseph resisted the sexual advances of his master's wife, and was thrown in prison for his efforts (Gen. 39:6-12). Joshua and Caleb tried to persuade the Israelites to have faith in God's power, and were nearly stoned to death. (Num. 14:1-10). Stephen preached the gospel, and was stoned to death (Acts 7). Paul preached the gospel, and was stoned, imprisoned, flogged, and harassed. John Huss preached the gospel in the commoner's language, and was burned at the stake. William Tyndale translated the Scriptures into the common language, and was strangled and burned. Today, in many areas of the world, those who choose to follow God and take His values as their own face punishment and even death.

other gods before me. You shall not make for yourself an idol in the form of anything in heaven above or on the earth beneath or in the waters below. You shall not bow down to them or worship them" (Deut. 5:7-10).

What, if any, values do you possess that are worth dying for?

Now that you have studied an example of the power of having strong, godly values and the impact they can have, it is time to begin examining and choosing the values you will allow to shape your life. Read Romans 6:1-23. In this chapter, Paul presented a contrast between two ways of living. He used several images to describe how a life is shaped and determined. One image pictures a king and his subjects. According to Romans 6:12, you should not allow _____ to be king in your life. Another image talks about volunteering to participate in something. According to Romans 6:13, you should not offer yourself as an instrument to _____, but rather offer yourself as an instrument to _____. The most powerful image he used is the concept of slavery. How would you describe the condition of a slave?

Slavery is a very powerful expression of how the values you hold, can consume and determine the very course of your life. According to Paul, you can choose to be a slave to _____, or a slave to _____. In Romans 6:16, Paul described the process by which you make your choice.

Rewrite verse 16 in your own words:

For the Christian, this choice should be automatic. In Romans 6:1-11, Paul described the effects of salvation. To trust in Jesus is, by definition, to turn away from the values and ways of sin and to accept the values and ways of God. Paul's whole argument in this chapter is that Christians ought not to live sinfully because Jesus has freed them from bondage of sin. When you examine your life, do you see evidence you are living according to the values and ways of sin, or the values and ways of God?

Paul also warned about the ultimate outcomes of this choice between two ways of living. Skim through Romans 6:1-23 and list the results of living for sin and living for God. Now, based on your study of Romans 6, as a Christian, what kind of values should be shaping your life?

Living for sin

Living for God

It is easy enough to discuss all this in the abstract. It becomes much more difficult when you begin to get specific. You have learned about two contrasting ways of living, two opposed sets of values on which to base your life. Take a moment and look back at the beginning of this study where you defined what a personal value is. With that definition in your mind, consider what you have learned about the two sets of values.

In the chart below, make a list of some of the values you think belong to the life of sin, and some of the values you think belong to the godly life.

Sin's Values

God's Values

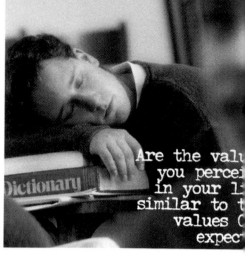

Are the valu
you percei
in your li
similar to t
values (
expect

God does not expect you to figure out His values on your own. He has provided much guidance. The way to discover the values God wants us to have is to study His Word. The following references are a selected list of Scripture passages that declare some of the values by which God expects His children to live. Read these Scriptures. On a separate sheet of paper, write simple statements of the values they express (you will find some values repeated in several passages; list them only once). A helpful way to state a value is to complete the phrase, "I should. . ."

Deuteronomy 5:6-21	Micah 6:8
Matthew 5:3-10	Matthew 22: 36-40
Matthew 28:19-20	John 15:1-14
Galatians 5:22-23	Ephesians 5: 8-10
Philippians 3:8	Colossians 3: 12-17
2 Peter 1:5-7	

Look back over the list of value statements you made. Think of at least one way the values can be expressed daily. For example, if the value is, "I should worship God," an expression of it might be, "I should spend time in prayer and praise each day."

Compare this list of values you found in Scripture with the values you expressed for your life at the beginning of this study. Are the values you perceive in your life similar to the values God expects?

Transformation. . . The goal of Bible study is different from much of the study you do. Bible study does not seek just to teach you information. Studying the Bible should lead to a transformation of your life. That is the unique power of God's Word. Hopefully, you have gained some information about values and their importance as you have completed this study. But a much more important goal is to allow that information to change your life. It is a choice to live by these newly discovered godly values and convictions.

What we choose to speak out for or against and the issues of life about which we choose to be silent give us clues to the values we hold. What things do you find yourself arguing for or against? During what kinds of discussions do you choose to keep your mouth shut?

What you do also reveals a great deal about what you value. To speak out about how wrong it is to steal but then to copy the answers to the test of the person sitting next to you says a lot about your values and your character.

If you are honest in your analysis, you might be dismayed to find out that the values your life reflects and the values you say you hold don't match up very well. Most people find this to be true. The solution to this dilemma is to make conscious decisions about the convictions of your life.

Look back at the list of values you found in your Scripture search. Using those statements as a reference, create a personal statement of the key values that you believe should be determining the course of your life as a Christian.

Key Values

If your life is going to reflect those values, what changes must be made? List some attitudes, behaviors, and activities that need to be discarded and others that need to be added.

Get Outta Here!

Let Me Have Some of That!

Now you know what you need to do. The only part that remains is to get to work doing it. Make an action plan for implementing those changes in your life. Set some realistic goals for specific steps you can take to accomplish the changes. Write your goals to complete the phrase, "I will . . ."

Now, pray! Ask God for the will and the strength to implement your plan and make your life one that counts.

David Tuten, youth minister and experienced youth curriculum writer from Alexander City, AL, is the writer of this lesson.

EXTRA CREDIT

1. Survey at least five spiritual people you respect and compile a list of their top five convictions or values they have.
2. Memorize Matthew 22:37–40.
3. Read the story "Service at Any Cost" on page 77 and some key values that feature suggest.
4. Identify one social issue debated today and write an essay either for or against from a biblical perspective.
5. Compile a list of at least 10 injustices or positive movements and identify some ways you can contribute to the cause of righteousness through them.

A Good Sense about Cents

Scripture Passages:
  Malachi 3:10;
  Matthew 25:14-30;
  2 Corinthians 8:1-5,7;
  Philippians 4:19
Lesson Truth: You honor God by investing in His kingdom.
Lesson Aim: To lead you to make the most out of your resources by:
  • describing how God blesses those who make investments in His kingdom.
  • investing your resources in the kingdom of God.

Consider the Source. . .

"Remember that time is money."
—Benjamin Franklin

"Put not your trust in money, but your money in trust."
—Oliver Wendall Holmes

"Ah, search the wide world wherever you can,
There is no open door for a moneyless man."
—Henry T. Stanton

"[The rich] are indeed rather possessed by their money than possessors."
—Robert Burton

"Money, which represents the prose of life, and which is hardly spoken of in parlors without an apology, is, in its effects and laws, as beautiful as roses."
—Ralph Waldo Emerson

It's not too hard to find an opinion on money. Whether you check out Bartlett's book of quotes or the latest issue of *Fortune* magazine, pieces of financial advice seem to come (pardon the pun) a dime a dozen.

With all that information floating across the television, radio, magazines, and Internet, sometimes it's hard to wade through the sea of facts and find a firm footing on what's solid.

Or is it? As Christians, we have the

greatest Source of all wisdom in God, and He provides that wisdom through His Word, the Bible. It only makes sense that we should take time to see what our Source has to say about the good and the bad of money.

Think about these questions, and record your answers in the space provided.

1. From where does the majority of my money come?

2. What am I most likely to do with the money I receive?

3. How quick am I to respond when I see a need I can help meet?

4. On a scale of 1-10, how would I rate my level of giving to God?

Robbing or Reaping. . .

Have you ever stolen something? If so, you probably understand the deep, haunting feeling that usually accompanies theft. It's especially true if you get caught—and even worse if you get caught red-handed!

Well, imagine stealing from God.

Hard to believe? Not really. In fact, the Bible provides a perfect example of a group of people—the ancient Jews—who were guilty of that very crime before God (Mal. 3:8-9).

The Jews had avoided paying the required "tithe" to God. Tithing, while mentioned only a handful of times in the Bible, was a common practice among the nations surrounding Israel.

But while their pagan neighbors were glad to make offerings to false gods, Israel had refused to be obedient in the area of giving to the only true God.

God called them on it. He called them "robbers" and even pronounced a curse upon those who refused to give Him the voluntary offering He deserved.

But that's not the end of the story. In Malachi 3:10, God contrasts the robbers by offering a pair of challenges and one mighty big blessing on the reapers—those who are obedient in their giving.

First, He tells the reapers to "bring the whole tithe into the storehouse." Translation: "Don't hold back. Don't go halfway in your commitment to me." If God can't trust you to go all the way for Him in your material giving, then He knows He won't be able to trust you with anything else either.

Second, He challenges the reapers to "test me in this." Translation: "Put your faith in Me. You can count on Me. I won't let you down." Everyone puts their faith in someone or something. Here, God is encouraging His followers to trust Him completely.

OK, so the reapers give all they've got and put their faith in God alone. What's the payoff?

"See if I [God] will not throw open the floodgates of heaven and pour out so much blessing that you will not have room enough for it" (Mal. 3:10).

The key to God's blessing rests in understanding "the floodgates of heaven." The Israelites thought of the sky as holding floodgates that God would open during the growing season to provide rain for the crops. That rain was their reward for acknowledging God's complete ownership and control of the land and the crops the land would produce. So, when God promised to open the floodgates for those who were obedient in their giving, the average Jew imagined a steady stream of life-giving rain.

It was complete blessing, including everything needed for growth and survival!

The danger in today's society is to hold back and not trust God, especially when the funds start running a little low. But, just like the Israelites, God holds a blessing for those who are obedient in giving.

Don't miss that word *obedient*. God's blessing is not so much attached to the gift or the act of giving as it is to the obedience of the giver. Do you honestly think God needs our money? Of course not! He doesn't want our money. He wants our obedience!

Think about some ways God challenges you in the area of giving. What are some areas where you have accepted His challenges? Where have you failed? What would it take to move you from being a robber to a reaper?

Using What You've Got. . .

Suppose you worked for a very wealthy man. Then, one day, he simply dropped a wad of cash on your desk and said, "I've got to help work out some kinks in the London office. Not sure how long it will take me—maybe months. Just do something with this for me while I'm gone and I'll check on it when I come back."

In the space below, write down what you would do with the boss' money while he was gone to London.

Well, you may never end up in that situation with your earthly boss; but, if you're a Christian, you're already in that position with your heavenly boss—God.

God has given us everything we have, including our money and other material possessions. Without His goodness, we wouldn't have a dime. But, beyond all that, God expects us to use the things He has given us to build His kingdom.

In a sense, He's dumped a load of cash on our table and said, "Do something with this for me while I'm gone, and I'll check on it when I come back." In Matthew 25:14-30, Jesus told a parable that emphasized this point. Take a few minutes and read about it.

A talent was the equivalent of about 20 years worth of work for the common Jew, so even the servant with one talent had a whole lot of money. Still, the master was not concerned as much with how much each servant was given. He cared more about the effort, commanding each of them to make the most of what he had given them while he was gone.

The first two servants were on the ball. By the time the master got back, each of them had doubled their investment. But the third servant was another matter altogether. Instead of making an investment, he simply "dug a hole in the ground and hid his master's money" (v. 18).

What happened when the master returned? The first two were praised for their hard work and investments. They were also put in charge of additional things and invited to share in the master's happiness (vv.

21, 23).

The third was not so fortunate. With the dirt still under his fingernails from digging up his master's cash, he plopped the money down. In a rage, the master ripped into the lazy servant, condemning his actions and giving his talent away to the one who had 10. "For everyone who has will be given more . . . whoever does not have, even what he has will be taken from him" (v. 29).

So, what's all this have to do with you? Before reading on, record some thoughts about the three servants and their master in the space below. Then, write down how you think this parable applies to your life.

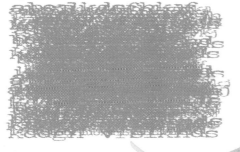

Obviously, Jesus is the Master and we fall into one of two categories of servants. He has given us much and we either use it for His glory or we refuse to invest it for Him. As in Malachi, God is looking for faithful and obedient servants who will take what they have (whether it's five talents or one talent) and use it to expand His work on earth.

Jesus doesn't force us to do anything with what He has given us. But like the master in the parable, He is coming back some day; and He will hold us accountable for what we have done with what we have been given.

Consider again how this parable might apply to your life. What are three practical things you can do to be a better caretaker of the resources God has given you? List them in the box provided.

1.
2.
3.

Giving with Grace. . .

Admittedly, giving is not one of the easier things to learn in the Christian life. Even though we know God expects us to give and even blesses those who give, it's tough to take our wallets out of our pockets and purses and put them in God's hands.

Even the apostle Paul had trouble convincing some of the members of his churches that giving was an important part of the Christian faith. In 2 Corinthians 8, Paul reminded the church in Corinth about a love offering he was collecting for the Christians in Jerusalem. The church in Jerusalem had suffered through some hard times, and many of the Gentile churches had happily pitched in to help their fellow Christians.

In addition, Paul may have hoped the monetary gift would help ease suspicions held by the Jews against him and the Gentile converts.

But he still faced one problem. The Christians in Corinth had not made good on the contribution they had promised for the Jerusalem church. Paul was having a tough time convincing them that giving was not only the right thing to do, it also was an outward sign of God's work in their lives. The Corinthians were not mature in their walk with God; and when a church struggles spiritually, it also struggles with its giving.

To support his case, Paul encouraged the Corinthians to take a look at their brothers and sisters in the surrounding areas of Macedonia, which is modern-day Greece. Each of those churches—such as, the Philippians, the Thessalonians, and the Bereans—had cheerfully given to the fund in the midst of difficulties.

Paul said these churches were enduring "a great ordeal of affliction" and "deep poverty," yet their giving "welled up in rich generosity" (v. 2). In other words, Paul said the Macedonians were like a beggar who had nothing and didn't expect to have anything, but still refused to let their circumstances hinder their generosity. Not only did they give, but they gave with such enthusiasm that Paul was blown away. They were literally begging "for the privilege of sharing" in the support of the saints (v. 4). Paul may have known about the Macedonian problems and urged them to be reasonable in their giving. But they begged to be included.

Author Warren Wiersbe has said that "circumstances will never be an

encouragement to give." In other words, no matter how well things go, our circumstances will always provide some sort of excuse for not giving obediently to God.

Have excuses been the only thing you've been giving God lately? Write your excuses for not giving in the space below.

Cheerful, excited giving—as displayed by the Macedonians—doesn't come naturally. In fact, it can only come supernaturally.

The only reason the Macedonian churches could be so joyful in spite of their circumstances was that they had acknowledged God's proper order for giving. First, they had given themselves completely to Him (v. 5). The Macedonians had made it a priority to confess that God owned everything; and, since everything was His, they were able to let go of it.

This "grace" in giving is what Paul encouraged the Corinthians to experience. He wanted the Christians in Corinth to live their faith through generous giving, which can only be explained in light of God's grace. He wanted them to "abound in this gracious work (of giving)" just as they had in the other areas (v. 7).

But it would not start until they completely committed all they had to Christ.

We are most like God when we give. List the things God has given

Without His goodness, we wouldn't have a dime.

you, beginning with His Son on the cross (John 3:16).

Consider the Source. . . If there was a natural question that would spring from Paul's letter, it would be this: If I sacrificially give everything I have to God, how will I meet my financial responsibilities?

That's a fair question—and Paul has the answer. It's nestled near the end of his short letter to the Philippians. (Remember, they were some of the cheerful givers who had sacrificed their resources to help the church in Jerusalem.)

In the latter verses of Philippians 4,

Paul thanked his friends in Philippi for their support of his ministry (vv. 14-17) and assured them he had all he needed (v. 18). Then he turned his attention to their troubles and said, "And my God will meet all your needs according to His glorious riches in Christ Jesus" (v. 19).

Sixteen little words, but their meaning must have powerfully encouraged the financially-strapped members of the Philippian church. His words should encourage us as well.

In that single, short verse, Paul summed up all the Bible's teaching on giving in four simple phrases:

1. "And my God." Who's the focus of everything? The One who is the Owner and Controller of everything. When you begin with God, you are destined for success. Paul understood this; so, from the start, he had the Philippians focus on Him.

2. "Will meet all your needs." Notice all the positive words in that

phrase. First, God "will." Paul didn't say "could" or "may" or "might" or "should." He said God will! No doubt about it! Second, "God will meet all." How much is all? All is all! Not part. Not some. All! Finally, he said "God will meet all your needs." Sometimes, we confuse our "needs" with our "greeds." But God doesn't commit Himself to providing our wishes or wants. We may not get all we would like, but we will never lack the things we truly need.

3. "According to His glorious riches." Again, God owns it all. His riches never run out. Whatever we need, He is more than able to supply.

4. "In Christ Jesus." Why would an all-powerful God take the time to meet our needs? Because we have a relationship with His Son—Christ Jesus! All that God does for the believer is based on that relationship. Jesus is the channel through which God meets every need!

The Philippians had been faithful to God, so God would be faithful to them. And He will be faithful to us, too.

Why do you think Paul could be so confident in turning the Philippians' attention back to God? What does it mean for God to be faithful? And, by the way, who is your Source?

The Payoff. . .
OK, so here's the Bible's scoop on giving. First, God expects it. Second, God blesses it. Third, God provides a supernatural desire to accomplish it. Fourth, God delivers for those who are faithful in it!

Any more questions? Take a look at the Book! The Bible is full of teachings and truths related to giving. Grab a concordance and some Bible study helps and dig a little deeper into His Word. While you're at it, ask God

to re-create you into the giver you should be!

Bob Bunn, youth curriculum editor for LifeWay Christian Resources of the Southern Baptist Convention, is the writer of this lesson.

EXTRA CREDIT

1. Determine how much you have given to the church and special offerings this last year. Set a goal to increase that amount this year.
2. Memorize Malachi 3:10.
3. Read the story "Budgeting and Stewardship" that begins on page 53 and do a budget sheet based on its suggestion.
4. Ask to sit in on your church's next stewardship or budget committee meeting. Take notes and seek to understand your church's financial system.
5. Make an anonymous donation to a special charity or ministry.

Budgeting and Stewardship

by Dr. Tony Rankin

Imagine yourself with no money. . . Visualize yourself with plenty of cash. . . Dream about yourself being a hermit. . . Think of yourself as an "overbooked," self-centered individual.

The above images may cause you to question the way you spend your time and money. As you enter a new phase of existence, it will be important to have a clear focus on how you budget your life. Wanting, spending, giving, and receiving are all good things when not taken to extremes. We were created to do each of them.

Warning from Steward General: Budget is not a bad word. Failure to have one could have life-threatening consequences.

Most people think that budget means inflexibility, guilt, harshness, ruthless, restrictions, and rigidity. Budget actually means balance. Finding a balance is another way to say, "in all your ways acknowledge him" (Prov. 3:6). All ways includes time and money. The first step to following this passage is learning how to choose a direction, make a plan, and implement the details.

In reality a budget is just a short-term spending and time management strategy. It is a process that will include estimating, allocating, costing, disbursement, and balance. It's the same concept as advanced planning for a vacation. Asking questions like, What do you want to do? How do you want to do it? Where are you going? will result in a more meaningful experience.

For one of the first times in your life, learning to demonstrate self-control will be totally your choice. No parental demands, stated preferences, rescuing you for their sake, or protecting you from poor choices. This is one of those see-I-can-do-it opportunities. Successful achievement with these opportunities makes you more desirable and marketable for future jobs and relationships. Start now with a Christlike approach for how you will "spend" your life.

Show Me the Money!

Although the expenses as a young adult are different from those of your parents, you need to get started setting good habits now. Some young adults use this spending formula: amount of paycheck = amount I spend this week.

The money in question to be spent may be a regular check you receive from a job, an on-going stipend from a college/university, or a systematic amount your parents provide for you. Regardless of the source of funds, use the following formula for your new spending routines.

Get in the habit of giving 10 percent to your church. It's much easier to learn to do so with a weekly income of $50 (giving $5 to your church) than it is to try to get used to making $1000 and trying to learn to give $100. It's not the amount you are giving that is significant—it's your attitude. Most churches can survive without your gifts but you can't afford not to give back to God.

Get used to saving at least 15 percent. This doesn't mean to save it until next month when the concert of the year comes to town. It means to save it for the future. There will be a day when you will need more money than you can find including when you decide to get married or buy a home. This does not mean hoarding—it means being prepared for something you don't fully understand or know yet. It means providing yourself with some security in addition to what your

Weekly Funds Total_____		Calculated Amounts
Tithe	10%	____
Savings	15%	____
Fun	20%	____
Debt	20%	____
Housing	25%	____
Necessities	10%	____

faith, family, friends, and reputation can provide.

Learn to live on a set amount of "fun" money. Don't allow it to exceed 20 percent of your paycheck or $30, which ever one is the least. This money can be used for eating out or an occasional movie. This will assist you in developing good habits when you get into the big adult world. Get cash from your paycheck and put it in your pocket (billfold or purse) or a special place at home, and don't spend a dime more than you have. If you have some left over, don't blow it! Save it for the next weekend or for the upcoming ticket to a special occasion.

Use or save 25 percent of your monies received for housing needs. If you live in the dorm or an apartment your parents provide for you, use these monies for necessary supplies for your living arrangements (i.e. vacuum cleaner, paper towels, cleaning supplies, light bulbs, lamps, etc.). If you don't use it, put it in your savings fund for future housing.

Use about 20 percent and any other funds you have left over to pay off debts with your parents, creditors, or school costs. Be aggressive with getting out of debt. The Scriptures say, "The borrower is servant to the lender" (Prov. 22:7). When you have these paid off, put the extra money with your savings and consider investing in mutual funds.

Use about 10 percent for necessities such as food, deodorant, oil changes for the car, and so forth.

Huge Hints

1. Have an emergency fund that could pay for at least your next semester's books or predicaments you might face in the next three months. Having $500 in an account offers a necessary sense of security that will prove to be a valuable asset.

2. Refuse to use the ATM (Automatic Teller Machine) or credit cards for fun money sources. This is how money disappears, checks bounce, impulsivity flourishes, debts increase, and frustration is birthed. Insignificant fund fees zap your fun monies.

3. Make your plans in detail so you understand how much things really cost and then have someone hold you accountable.

I Got the Time!

A Nashville, Tennessee school building wall is painted with the acrostic T.I.M.E.—Today I Must Excel! Time is something of which everyone has equal amounts. It's the thing we want the most but use the worst. Time is associated with work and play.

The opposite of work is not "having fun." It is idleness, which involves not investing yourself in anything. Learning to genuinely invest self can include finding direction with various life areas: academic, vocation, physical, spiritual, relationships, and family.

Helpful Hints

If you will be a college student, plan on studying at least one hour for every hour in class. In other words, if you are taking 13 hours plan on spending 13 hours studying during the week—preferably during normal waking hours and not all day on Saturday or Sunday. Studying on a daily basis will prove extremely beneficial

academically, socially, and physically.

Find a balance in studying alone and in groups. Do whichever can be most productive academically.

After the first two weeks of the semester, devise a plan and live by a set schedule. Suggestion: Don't do anything but sleep between 12–7 a.m. Utilize the other 17 hours for studying, eating, socializing, dating, reading, working, and going to class. Studies show that minimal material is retained or learned at 3:00 a.m.

Limit your employment as much as possible. If you are attending classes full-time and you want those hours to be meaningful and helpful, limit your employment to 14 hours. This will allow you time to study, prepare for tests and write papers, and have a suitable social life. If at all possible try to work on campus for the convenience, understanding, and flexibility. Remember, you are in college to be educated, learn about life, and obtain wealth—in that order. Of course, if you are putting yourself through school and/or having to support your family, this guideline will need to be adjusted.

Set an amount of hours to do service or mission projects, personal Bible study, and spiritual growth. Spending five hours a week doing such will strengthen your walk with Christ.

Being a good manager of your time and money will be manifested like Matthew 25:21. This passage says, "His master replied, 'Well done, good and faithful servant! You have been faithful with a few things; I will put you in charge of many things. Come and share your master's happiness!'"

Tony Rankin is a long-time youth minister and Christian counselor in Nashville, TN.

Second Chance

You Can't Go Back. . . In the three *Back to the Future* movies, teenager Marty McFly and mad scientist Emmit "Doc" Brown jump back and forth to the past, present, and future so many times it's difficult to keep up with them. All that's necessary for them to do this is to hop into Doc's plutonium-powered car-turned-time machine and punch in any date and time they wish. Interestingly, though, did you ever notice that in no matter what time period they found themselves, they were always faced with the dilemma of fixing something so the future wouldn't be altered? They spent most of their time, it seems, pondering how to remedy the mistakes Doc's time machine caused.

Wouldn't it be great to be able to hop into a time machine and go back to the past? You could right your wrongs, make the best choices this time, and get a fresh start. Well, there's good news and bad news concerning this. First, the bad news: even in our highly-advanced scientific age, they still haven't created a machine that can take you back in time, nor will they ever be able to do so. Now, the good news: you do get second chances with God! In fact, the best second chances you get are from God. You may have never considered this, but that's what God offers us every time we mess up. His second chances affect how we live the rest of

Scripture Passages:
2 Samuel 11:1-16
Psalm 51; 103:11-12
John 13:37-38
18:15-27
2 Corinthians
5:15-21;
1 John 1:8-10;
Lesson Truth: God can use you regardless of your past.
Lesson Aim: To lead you to accept God's forgiveness by:
• acknowledging that God can use you regardless of your past mistakes.
• committing to being a representative of Christ in your daily life.

an I still make a difference even though I have made mistakes in my past?

our lives and where we will spend our future for eternity.

This study will hopefully lead you to see how to go about getting second chances with God, and how you can take advantage of the opportunity you have in your life right now—even with the past mistakes you've made—to make a fresh start and allow God to use you as you make the transition to life beyond high school.

Right now, just for fun, write one mistake you've made in the past that you would change if you had a time machine.

Now, mark through it and write what you would do now in that situation given a second chance. Granted, getting a second chance to right that wrong won't be as easy as just marking through it, but with God—who is a God of second chances—anything is possible!

Biblical Second-Chancers. . .

Sometimes, you may feel as though the mistakes you've made in the past are the worst ones ever committed. You're probably still embarrassed about some of them. But cheer up! Ordinary people in the Bible, as well as God's best and brightest, made what even we would consider some real blunders. Look up the following verses, then jot down who the biblical character was and the mistake(s) made:

2 Samuel 11:1-16:

John 13:37-38; 18:15-27:

Acts 7:54-8:3:

Luke 15:11-16:

Yes, it was David who committed adultery with another man's wife, then murdered her husband by having him put on the battlefield where he would be killed. "Bold" Peter denied Christ three times—publicly—even though he promised Jesus he could never do that. Saul's life crusade was persecuting followers of Christ in any way he could. In the parable of the prodigal son, the young man blew his inheritance—his father's hard-earned money—on all the sinful pleasures he could find. If you're keeping score, that's one sin of adultery (David), one count of murder (David, again), one bad case of turning your back on your leader and best friend (Peter), several counts of harassment, battery, and probably attempted murder (Saul), and several indictments of drinking, soliciting prostitutes, and general wild living (the prodigal son). If anyone needed a second chance, it was these guys. But if you haven't figured it out already, they all got second chances.

David, after being confronted by the prophet Nathan, repented. Look at what David later wrote as recorded in Psalm 51. What was his response?

Peter also got a second chance. Even though he turned his back on Christ along with everyone else, Jesus didn't turn His back on Peter. Look at John 21:15-19 to see how Jesus reinstated Peter and challenged him to carry on the work yet to be done.

Saul turned his life around after God got his attention on the way to Damascus. Saul was headed there, of course, to hassle more Christians. Read Acts 9:1-6,17-22 and check out the transformation in his life.

The prodigal son got an opportunity for a fresh start after he returned to his father in humility. Even though he had wasted all his father had given him, look at the father's response in Luke 15:17-24.

These few examples go to show us these guys were all in bad shape before they got a second chance. But what does this have to do with me? you may be asking. Well, unless you're perfect, you need second chances, too. And even if you do suffer from some of the same types of sin these guys exhibited, remember: there's hope because our God is a God of second chances.

Second Chance "Inventory". . .

Let's spend just a moment looking at your past, because as they say, the past is prelude to the future. In this sense, that means you will probably keep doing the same types of things in the future as you have done in the past; unless, of course, you trust and depend on God's strength to chart out a new future.

Now, let's do something interesting. This is not for the purpose of dredging up your past mistakes; it's for the purpose of showing you something about yourself. Rate the following statements from 1 to 5, with 1 being "strongly disagree" and 5 being "strongly agree."

1 2 3 4 5 I can never have a really great future because of the mistakes I have made in the past.

1 2 3 4 5 I have a bad—or less than ideal—reputation that seems to follow me wherever I go.

1 2 3 4 5 I am often reminded (either by others or by my own thoughts) of the bad choices I have made in the past.

1 2 3 4 5 I don't really see the need to try to improve from my past failures. I can't help who or what I am.

1 2 3 4 5 I'm not to blame for the bad choices I've made in the past. It was someone else's fault.

Now, let's analyze your responses. Add up your total score and write it here: _____ (Maximum of 25 points)

Even though this is not a scientific, foolproof way to tell if your future may be altered because of your past, there is a good indication that the following statements, based on your score, may apply to you.

If you scored 1–7, you likely have a very good past with no regrets. (Second chances? Who needs 'em?)

If you scored 8–13, you have a past that you can probably still be proud of. There are no "skeletons in your closet" to haunt you— at least, none of any size. (Second chances? I can live without them.)

If you scored 14–19, you likely have some fairly bad past mistakes. You've probably "blown it" a few times. (Second chances? I could use some.)

If you scored 20–25, it's pretty definite you have a

painful past that could lead to a painful future unless you get off the road you're on. (Second chances? My whole life depends on them!)

Whether this mental exercise was painful or pleasant for you, there is a lesson to be learned. If you had a good grade on the test (a low number), by all means keep up the good work! God can really use people like you. However, never forget you may one day need a chance to start over. Even if you do, God can take your mistake and turn it into a learning and growing experience for you.

On the other hand, if you had what was considered a not-so-great grade on the test (a high number), don't despair. The game is not yet over! You may be trailing the other team at the end of high school, but you can regroup and come out on top as a young adult if you accept the forgiveness God offers you.

Seeking forgiveness, though, can be especially hard because it means admitting we have done something wrong.

Forgiveness: Necessary for Starting Over. . .

There are two things that are very difficult to do but are necessary to start over. One of them is to seek forgiveness. When God forgives you for a past mistake, you don't have to worry about dwelling on that sin again; then you can really change! Psalm 103:11-12 tells us how much God loves us (the distance between heaven and the earth) and how fully He removes our sins (as far as the east is from the west). What a promise. What a motivation for change to take place. Imagine how great God is, then think about how strong His forgiveness must be to forget what we have done. We may forgive, but we can't forget. However, God can!

Seeking forgiveness, though, can be especially hard because it means admitting we have done something wrong. It's hard for most people to do that. In fact, most people think it makes them look weak when they have to admit they're not perfect. But that's exactly what we have to do if we want to humbly seek the forgiveness God offers. There are specifically two kinds of forgiveness we must seek.

Salvation.—The first kind of forgiveness God desires for us to seek from Him is the most important kind. It is the forgiveness you seek when you realize you are lost in sin and separated from God unless you accept the forgiveness offered from Him through His Son, Jesus. You may fit into this category right now. If so, no matter what you've done or where your life has taken you, Jesus waits with open arms to forgive you! God paid a high price for this type of forgiveness; He sent His Son as a sacrifice. But it is impossible for you to get second chances with God unless you first deal with this. See the inside cover of this book for information about the plan of salvation. If you do make this decision and pray to accept God's forgiveness, be sure to share it with someone who can help you follow through and get "plugged in" as a Christian so God can use you from this point forward.

Recommitment.—Many of you, however, have already made a decision regarding your salvation. The second kind of forgiveness, then, that is part of God's second-chance plan involves asking His forgiveness in what is called recommitment. It means going to God and reaffirming your decision to live for Him. First John 1:8-10 tells us that even though we are all sinners, we can be forgiven of every sin if we confess them to God. There may be no better time in life for you to do this than right now! That's because, sadly, many youth "drop through the cracks" of the church floor after high school. Whether they go to college or into the work force, this newfound freedom and the ability to make their own decisions causes them to leave God out of their lives. It should be sobering for you to consider that it is possible— even if you are a strong Christian—to begin living a life of inconsistency on the college campus, in a job, in the military, or in whatever path life takes you after high school. Even if you have messed up in high school, now is the time to get past that and allow God to change you. Take advantage of God's second chance plan now!

Change: Another Necessity for Starting Over. . . The other tough thing in starting over is the change that will be necessary. When we're accustomed to doing something a certain way, it really is tough to relearn it. We usually resist change, and that goes for immoral lifestyles, bad habits, and ungodly actions, too. Changing these things is tough, and our sinful nature may really rebel against change—even positive change.

Think for a minute: What are some changes or adjustments you have already had to make in life?

Which were especially painful?

Have there been any changes or adjustments you have had to make that ended up helping you become a better person? If so, what?

Change will be a natural result if God is really in control of your life. I'm not talking about the change-because-it-will-look-good variety or the change-is-supposed-to-happen-when-you-recommit mindset, but change resulting because you are allowing God to control your life. With radical forgiveness on God's part comes the ability to change and move ahead on our part.

Look Out for the Forgiveness "Traps"...

Assuming you are about to plunge off into college, work, or whatever you see as God's plan for your future, there's no better time to "make like a snake" (shed your old skin for a new one). Now, the hard part: How? Isn't it enough to just have positive thoughts? For example, "Now that I'm going off to college, no one there will know my past and I'll just start over by being a strong Christian." There's absolutely nothing wrong with having those kinds of ideals. However, it also doesn't take a genius to figure out it won't be that easy. There's a good possibility you could be back to your old way of life before you even know your way around the college campus. Sure, you have good intentions, but they can quickly evaporate on an exciting college campus filled with lots of temptations for young students trying to get off to a good start.

What kinds of traps do you expect to find in your near future that will make starting over difficult? Here are a few pitfalls. Circle these and/or feel free to add more of your own.

Alcohol/Drugs
Gambling
Material Possessions
Cheating
Sex
Spiritual Apathy
Pornography
Relationships
Time Management
Others that relate especially to you:

Take advantage of God's second chance plan now!

Along with these traps, a word of warning needs to be added about forgiveness. Even though you have accepted God's forgiveness for your past mistakes doesn't mean you are to face the next day with the attitude that, "Hey, if I mess up again, it's no big deal; I'll just go back to God, ask for forgiveness, and then go back to living the way I want." That's a dangerous trap in which to get caught! Sin is always a big deal to God. He desires true sorrow for the way we have acted. When we truly repent of our sins, that means we turn 180 degrees from the way we were going. In other words, we turn away from our sinful actions and turn to God. What good does it do if we get caught in the cycle of sin, forgiveness, sin, forgiveness, and so on? Not only does God know we are not sincere, it's also going to make us spiritually miserable and unable for God to use us.

Are there things you have seen in others' lives that make them miserable because they are trapped in the sin, forgiveness, sin, forgiveness cycle? List them:

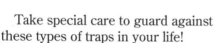

1.

2.

3.

Take special care to guard against these types of traps in your life!

One Day at a Time. . .

This may all sound very good to you, but on the other hand, it may sound a little overwhelming. If it does, you're not alone. A boy in our youth group (who had the tendency to take a step backwards spiritually every now and then) came to me one night at camp with a tough question. He had just made a recommitment and asked how he could make it last. The best advice I could offer him was this: "You can do it if you take things one day at a time." That's also the best advice to offer you now. If you look at the big picture and think about living a godly life for the rest of your life, the awesomeness of that may blow your mind and you may think, *There's no way I can do this! Why even try?* However, if you focus on today only, it will seem very possible to live for God. Tomorrow, you do the

same thing; then, the day after.

If we can put our past behind us and not glance back at it, it follows that God can then use us. Being used by God! Isn't that awesome to think about? Not only do we get our sins forgiven and get a second chance, but on top of that we actually have the privilege of being used by God and joining Him in the work He is doing in the world. We are sinful, and we always will be; yet, the perfect, all-present, all-powerful, and all-knowing Creator of the universe desires to forgive us and use us in His work. Take advantage of God's second-chance plan!

Tan Flippin, youth curriculum editor at LifeWay Christian Resources of the Southern Baptist Convention, is the writer of this lesson.

EXTRA CREDIT

1. Write a prayer to God asking for forgiveness in an area where you have blown it.
2. Memorize 2 Corinthians 5:17.
3. List as many examples in the Bible as you can where God gave people a second chance.
4. Read Ephesians 2. Make a list of all the things you were before salvation and make another list of all the things you are now in Christ.
5. Find an accountability partner with whom you can pray and confess regularly.

A Friend Is a Friend in Deed

Think about the people you call your friends. How did they become your friends? You didn't just pick their names out of a hat. You probably enjoy spending time with them. You probably agree on things and have a lot of ideas in common. Some of these friends may have been a part of your life since early elementary school. You've grown up together. Other friends may have come into your life in recent years. Even though the situations may vary some, these friends are people you can trust.

Here's a tougher question: How much do you let God be a part of your friendships? Sometimes we tend to put the different areas of our lives into compartments. For example we have school and home and church and sports and music and friends. Maybe you have some different compartments in your life. Sometimes these parts of our lives remain unrelated. We want to keep God in a neat little package we open up each Sunday or when we have an emergency and really need Him. Do you know God wants to be involved in every area of your life, and that

> **Scripture Passages:**
> 1 Samuel 20;
> Proverbs 17:17; 12:26;
> 2 Corinthians 6:14
> James 4:4;
>
> **Lesson Truth:** You can follow God's principles for relationships.
> **Lesson Aim:** To lead you to follow God's principles for relationships by:
> • determining godly principles for relationships.
> • committing to have relationships that are positive influences in your life.

includes your friendships? He would like to be a part of your decisions when choosing new friends and a part of your relationships with friends you already have.

As a soon to be graduate, this is probably a turning point in your life where you say goodbye to some friends who are leaving for college or military service. You'll also be saying hello to some new friends as you meet them in these new situations. This study will help you understand God's principles for all of our relationships with the people we call "friends."

Choosing Friends. . .

When you were younger, your parents had tremendous influence over your friendships. They pretty much decided who you played with and when and where you played. Now that you border young adulthood, everything has changed. Now you will make the decisions about your friendships. Remember, God has a plan for your life and that includes your friendships. Here's how you can let God guide your choice of friends:

Choose Your Friends Carefully.—Think about the amount of time you spend choosing clothes and hairstyles. Do you spend that much time choosing friends? Friends are an important part of our lives. They influence us and we influence them. So when you are choosing new friends, it's wise to think carefully about their language, attitudes, and actions before you decide to invest a lot of time in the relationship.

Take a look at Proverbs 12:26 and 2 Corinthians 6:14. What are the warnings in these verses?

If you have a friend who is involved in activities that would be displeasing and disobedient to God, then what are the dangers for you in this relationship?

There are people whose lifestyles go against God's plan for living.

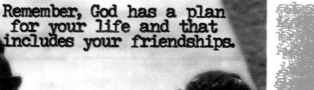

Remember, God has a plan for your life and that includes your friendships.

Becoming friends with a person like that could ultimately draw you away from God's will for your life. The Bible does not teach we should never have anything to do with people who are unbelievers. The Bible instructs us to be salt and light in our world. There may be times when your Christian example could be a positive influence in a friend's life. But the Bible also teaches we

JERRY GAZA

should be cautious about getting involved in any close relationships that might weaken our Christian beliefs.

List some of the qualities you like to find in your friends:

1.
2.
3.
4.

Do you have these same qualities in your life?

Let God Guide Your Choice.— Sometimes we forget God is interested in the small details of our lives. We pray and ask for His help in the big things, like sickness, death, or divorce. Have you ever prayed and asked for God's guidance in finding new friends? If we don't allow God to guide our choices, then we run the risk of friendships that could damage our relationship with God.

Read James 4:4. What do you think it means to have "friendship with the world"?

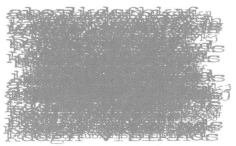

If we are looking for entertainment and friends that keep us from pleasing God, then those friendships are wrong. As you prepare to go to college, the military, or the workplace, you'll be meeting lots of new people. Some of the people will have personalities that are exciting and attractive, but their lifestyles are in conflict with God's teachings. Ask God to lead you to the friends He would

want you to have. If you spend time reading the Bible, praying, and looking for God's direction concerning your friendships, then He will lead you in the right direction.

Keeping Friends. . . We've seen that the Bible has something to say about the friends we choose. The Bible also has something to say about the characteristics of a good, strong friendship. One of the best examples of friendship is found in the Old Testament between David and Jonathan. Remember Jonathan's father, Saul, was king of Israel. David was the man God had chosen to be the next king of Israel. Jonathan and David were best friends, but when we read 1 Samuel 20, we find that their friendship faced a difficult test.

As he grew older, Saul became very jealous of David, to the point that he wanted to kill David. Jonathan must have been torn between loyalty to his father and his friendship with David. In spite of these difficulties, Jonathan and David remained loyal friends. Let's take a look at their friendship to see what made it strong enough to withstand so many troubles.

Real Friends Are Dependable. . . When David first told Jonathan King Saul was trying to kill him, Jonathan could not believe it. So David devised a plan that required Jonathan's help. Jonathan would make an excuse to his father that David could not be present for dinner the next day. If Saul became angry when he heard the news, then Jonathan and David would know for sure Saul wanted to kill David. If Saul was not angry, then they would know David was wrong about Saul's desires. You'll find their plan in 1 Samuel 20:4-8.

Jonathan told David, "Whatever you want me to do, I'll do for you" (v. 4). Dependability is important. Think about the people we count on each day to keep their word: parents, teachers, family members, and friends. If we cannot depend on a person or that person cannot depend on us, then we really shouldn't even call it friendship. There's no such thing as shallow friendship. Real friends know they can count on each other.

Think about a time when you have faced some trial or difficulty. Did you have a friend there to help? Write a sentence describing your dependence on them.

Have you been available to help a friend who was going through a hard time? Write a sentence describing your assistance.

As a soon-to-be-graduate, this is probably a turning point in your life where you say goodbye to some friends who are leaving for college or military service.

Sadly, sometimes we find out who our real friends are during hard times. Maybe someone you thought was a friend let you down when you really needed help. You may have many acquaintances—the people who sit beside you in class or a neighbor who lives nearby. But true friends are ready and available to help in good times and difficult times. You can count on your friends and they can count on you.

Real Friends Are Giving. . .

Jonathan was the king's son and David was accusing the king of some awful things. Jonathan could have said, "shut up!" because David was talking about his father and also his king. But Jonathan was willing to listen to all the facts and then, seeing his father's evil behavior, chose to remain loyal to David. In 1 Samuel 20:13-17 you'll find the promise Jonathan and David made to each other to remain loyal and true, no matter what the circumstances.

Real friends are willing to give. Think about your best friend. What are the things you "give" to

this relationship? What does your friend "give" to the relationship?

A friendship that only goes one way doesn't last very long. Sometimes a person enjoys all the benefits of a friendship, but is never willing to give anything in return. A strong friendship takes two people willing to give to each other. If one person is always giving while the other person is always taking, then it isn't a true friendship and it doesn't last very long.

Jonathan and David made specific promises to each other about how they would treat each other because they were friends. Have you ever been involved in a situation where one friend got mad at another because some expectations were unclear? Maybe one friend just assumed the other would do a certain thing. When it wasn't done, feelings were hurt. Real friends spend time talking to each other so the lines of communication are clear and open. Then it's less likely misunderstandings will occur.

Verse 17 reads, "And Jonathan had David reaffirm his oath out of love for him, because he loved him as he loved himself."

What does it mean to love a friend like you love yourself? How can you show your love to your friends?

Real Friends Take Positive Risks for Each Other. . .

Just as David thought, Saul was extremely angry when Jonathan told him David would not be present for the meal. Saul spoke angry words at Jonathan, saying Jonathan would never be king as long as David was alive. In spite of Saul's anger, Jonathan questioned his father, asking, "Why should he be put to death? What has he done?" These questions made Saul so angry he threw his spear at Jonathan in an attempt to kill him. Jonathan was angry and sad about his father's feelings toward David. You'll find this story in 1 Samuel 20:31-34.

It would have been easier for Jonathan to break off his relationship with David. Then his father wouldn't be so angry with him. But Jonathan was willing to take a risk for the sake of their friendship. Sometimes being a friend requires you to sacrifice and maybe even endure hardship for that friend.

Jonathan was willing to take risks for his friend David. Can you name some examples of positive risks you may have taken for a friend? Are you willing to take risks for your friends?

Taking risks doesn't mean going along with friends doing foolish, risky things. Think about the following situations:

Your friend Felicia has a boyfriend who has gotten into a lot of trouble. Her parents object to her seeing him. Felicia wants you to tell her parents she was with you when she was actually out with her boyfriend.

Your friend Robby has to get a B on tomorrow's math test in order to pass the class. He sits next to you and you're an A student. Robby suggested you leave your test uncovered so he can see your answers.

Your friend Karyn was caught shoplifting some makeup items from a department store. You were with her in the store. She wants you to say she already owned the items when you know she took them from the counter.

Even though you might feel pressure to "help" your friend, what is the best way you can be a friend in these situations?

Real Friends Don't Quit...

After Saul threw the spear in anger, Jonathan could have decided he didn't need to be in the middle of this mess between his father and David. We would understand if Jonathan had chosen not to see David anymore because of all the difficulties.

But Jonathan didn't quit. He kept his promise to meet David and warn him that Saul did want to kill him. You'll find their promise of friendship in verse 42 as Jonathan said to David, "Go in peace, for we have sworn friendship with each other in the name of the LORD, saying, 'The LORD is witness between you and me, and

between your descendants and my descendants forever.'" We know they kept this promise, because later on the Bible says David cared for Jonathan's son even after Jonathan's death.

At this time in their lives, when it would have been easier for Jonathan and David to give up on their friendship, they refused to quit.

List some of the difficult situations you have faced with your friends.

What is the key to keeping a friendship together in difficult times?

As you look ahead to college, new jobs, or the military, it may be that you're going to be physically separated from your friends. Being apart can sometimes put a strain on a relationship. But a friendship doesn't have to end just because someone moves away. How can you keep a friendship strong even when you're physically apart from the person?

Think about phone calls, e-mail, letters, or visits. These things can help keep a friendship connected when the miles separate you.

Read Proverbs 17:17. Maybe you've heard the expression "fair weather friend." It's a person who wants to be your friend when the sun is shining—when everything is going well. But when things go wrong (bad weather), then this "fair weather friend" disappears. Maybe you've had to learn the hard way some people aren't really the friends you thought. Read each of the following situations and then write a short answer telling how you would respond as a "friend" in the situation.

Mark's parents are getting a divorce. He's sad to see his family breaking up and he's discouraged because of all the arguing that goes on between his parents.

Alicia's dad got a new job and her family now has to move to another state. She's sad to leave behind all her church friends and school friends.

You and Alex were both excited about trying out for the school track team. You made the team, but Alex did not.

There are some nasty rumors circulating around school about Natalie. She denies them, but there are people still talking behind her back.

Ramon's younger sister is sick and in the hospital. The doctors are running tests to find out what's wrong. Ramon's whole family is very worried about her and Ramon finds it difficult to think about anything but his sister.

Growing Friendships— God's Way. . .

Being a good friend is kind of like growing a plant. You can stick a seed in some dirt and just leave it alone. Maybe it will grow a little bit. But eventually it will die. The seed will never grow into a strong healthy plant unless you water it, place it where it receives sunshine, and fertilize it.

Friendships require some tender loving care—just like plants. The water and sunshine of dependability, trust, honesty, and loyalty will help your friendships grow strong and healthy like the plant. The strongest, healthiest friendships will be planted in God's love. God desires the best for you in every area of your life. This includes your friendships too.

Donna McKinney, youth worker and experienced youth curriculum writer in White Plains, MD, is the writer of this lesson.

EXTRA CREDIT

1. Make a list of your closest friends and rank the friendship on a scale of 1-10 with 10 being perfect. Next to each name list some things you can do to make the relationship stronger.
2. Memorize Proverbs 17:17.
3. List the qualities you desire in a friend. Check off those qualities you try to express in your friendships.
4. Find a good Christian book on relationships and read it. Apply some of the principles to your relationships.
5. Look for opportunities to establish two new friendships in the next month.

Making It My Busines

Have you ever heard a rumor or observed a friend involved in an activity you felt should be confronted?

Your friend is involved in an activity that has you really worried. He has not talked to you about it. Others have told you what they have seen and heard. You have seen a change in his personality that has not been good.

In the space below write down what you would do or how you would handle this situation.

Scripture Passages:
    2 Samuel 12:1–14;
    Galatians 2:11–16;
Lesson Truth: You are to encourage others to do the right thing.
Lesson Aim: To lead you to encourage others by:
    • summarizing Nathan's confrontation with David and Paul's confrontation with Peter.
    • determining principles for confronting others.

Confronting a friend is never easy. If you do not handle the situation correctly, you risk losing the friendship. You walk a very fine line between what is best for your friendship and making something your business that is not any of your business. How do you determine when you need to confront a friend? What is the best way to address your concern? Is it your responsibility to encourage other people to do the right thing?

David, the psalmist and king of Israel, appeared to have everything going for him. God had given him a great job as king. His resume included some very impressive victories—everything from slaying a nine foot giant to defeating entire armies. His friends were willing to put their lives and reputations on the line for him. He was a great looking guy with a beautiful and devoted wife. God was continually blessing David. David was a man after God's own heart. Everything was looking good for David. Then he blew it in a big way.

One evening David was out strolling on the roof of his home. From his rooftop he saw Bathsheba. Bathsheba was the wife of Uriah, a man who served in David's army. Bathsheba was a beautiful woman. David, carried away by what he saw that night, had an adulterous affair with Bathsheba and she became pregnant. By this time, David's relationship with God was at an all-time low. David's sins grew rapidly. Lust led to adultery. Adultery led to a pregnancy. An unwanted pregnancy led to the deception of Uriah that ultimately ended in David's order to have Uriah murdered.

OK, you have the facts. What would you do? If David were your friend, how would you approach him? Read 2 Samuel 12:1-14 to see how the prophet Nathan confronted David. What motivated Nathan to confront David?

How did Nathan lead David to a clear understanding of the sin in David's life?

What was David's first reaction to Nathan's parable?

Nathan told David he was the guilty man. What was David's reaction to Nathan's confrontation?

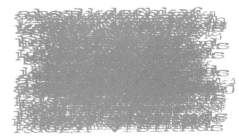

Nathan put his own life in jeopardy when he confronted David. Can you imagine confronting the President of the United States or someone else who is in a position of authority over you? You will need courage when the time comes for you to confront a friend. Even though it is difficult, it is sometimes necessary. Confrontation serves to lead a person away from mediocrity or to lead one back from extremes in their behavior.

How Do You Know if It's Your Place to Confront a Friend?

Do not jump to conclusions. Make sure there is a problem. Do not make assumptions based upon hearsay. Look for signs in your friend that will confirm your suspicions. Have you noticed a change in his or her behavior? Have you noticed him or her being more aggressive or angry? Oftentimes people try to deal with hurt, anger, or embarrassment in their lives by lashing out. This is often a sign something is wrong.

Have you noticed that your friend is not hanging out with other people the way he or she once did? Maybe your friend is very busy or maybe he or she has a new circle of friends. If you notice your friend is spending unusual amounts of time alone, this may not be a good sign. You may need to be concerned if your friend is not participating in activities he or she once enjoyed or if your friend is neglecting his or her other friends. For example, a very outgoing person who begins to withdraw may be dealing with some kind of stress in his or her life.

Has your friend been more moody lately than normal? Let's face facts; some people are moodier than others. That's just the way we are. During the teenage years there is so much going on physically, emotionally, and spiritually that moodiness is naturally going to happen. What you need to be aware of are mood swings that seem overboard. If you notice that your friend's moodiness is more frequent and the mood swings more severe than normal, this may indicate a problem.

Do you know of any major life problems your friend may be having? The breakup of a relationship, health problems, family issues, financial problems, poor grades, and many other major trauma can trigger behavior in people that might not, under normal conditions, be normal.

After carefully and prayerfully assessing the situation, you may feel it is not your responsibility to confront your friend. It may be that it is too painful for you to deal with. You may think the situation will take care of itself without any intervention from you. Be certain your decision not to confront is not a selfish decision. If you do not take the time, energy, and responsibility to talk with a friend whom you love, who will? Do not let pride or insecurity keep you from doing what needs to be done.

What's Your Motivation for Confrontation?

If, after looking at the situation and praying about it you know you need to talk with your friend, here are some things to consider:

Make certain your motivation for confrontation is pure. Ask yourself why you feel you need to talk with your friend. If you are motivated by selfishness, you need to rethink your desire to confront. Revenge is also never a reason to approach someone. Even if they have hurt or disappointed you, you are to respond in love.

Read John 21. During the trial of Jesus, Peter denied being a disciple three times. How did Jesus confront Peter? What was Jesus' motivation for talking to Peter?

Oftentimes people try to deal with hurt, anger, or embarrassment in their lives by lashing out.

If you are motivated by anything other than what is best for the person you feel you need to confront, then your motives and heart may be in the wrong place.

Make certain your motivation is based on love and concern. When you confront a person and they do not sense you genuinely care for them, the tendency is to become defensive or angry. Be sure your friend understands you are talking with them because you love them and desire the very best for them. Your friend needs to understand that you believe their activity in wrong; however, you still care for them. Caring should always come first. Confronting comes after a sense of caring is established.

In John 4:1-42, Jesus confronted a Samaritan woman. Read this passage. What was the Lord's motivation for confronting this woman? Do you think she felt the love and concern Jesus had for her?

Jesus' love and concern for the Samaritan woman was overwhelmingly obvious to her. She sensed His motivation was to make certain her life was on track. He could have easily come down very hard on her. He could have pointed out that compared to His holiness and righteous living she really was in bad shape. However, Jesus didn't condemn her. He loved her. She experienced love that day in a way she had never experienced love before.

Make certain you do not come across to the other person as being more spiritual or "holier than thou."

Confrontation
happens. Sometimes
it is a positive
experience.
Sometimes it is a
negative experience.

Make certain your motivation is from God. When you talk to people, you have a responsibility as a Christian to respond to them in the same way Jesus would respond to them. Have you ever heard the saying, "You may be the only Jesus people ever see"? Be sure that when you confront a friend they see and hear the love of Christ coming through loud and clear.

Guidelines for Confrontation. . .

Confronting a friend is not easy but it is probably inevitable. Confrontation happens. Sometimes it is a positive experience. Sometimes it is a negative experience. The guidelines below will help you to be a more sensitive and caring confronter.

• Prayerfully confront.—There will never be a situation or circumstance you will encounter in your life that does not call for prayer. Throughout the gospels we see examples of how Christ bathed His entire life and ministry in prayer. In John 17, Jesus prayed an incredible prayer for protection for His disciples. He prayed they would be made ready to serve God through truth.

Before you confront your friend, pray for him or her. Pray that God will reveal His truth and His wisdom. If your friend is a Christian, the Holy Spirit of God abides within his or her heart. It is not your right or your responsibility to convict people of their sin. God will deal with His people in His own way.

Before you confront your friend, pray for yourself. Pray you are seeing the situation the way it really is. You need to remain objective as you talk. You need to have a good attitude. If this person has hurt you or has become your enemy, Matthew 5:44 commands us to pray so that our relationship with the Father is what it needs to be. Pray for discernment. It is of the utmost importance that your friend realize you are talking to him or her out of a desire to help. Pray that as you talk with him or her you will express genuine care and concern.

As you are talking to your friend, you will need to be in constant communication with God. His leadership in this situation is not an option. Lean on His understanding and His knowledge.

You may want to consider praying with your friend. If you are both believers, you need to pray together about the situation. Prayer brings peace to a situation. Peace replaces worry. Philippians 4:6-7 says, "Do not be anxious about anything, but in everything, by prayer and petition, with thanksgiving, present your requests to God. And the peace of God, which transcends all understanding, will guard your hearts and your minds in Christ Jesus."

• Calmly confront.—If you appear to be angry or overly upset, the natural tendency is for the person being confronted is to become angry and defensive. Proverbs 15:1 says, "A gentle answer turns away wrath, but a harsh word stirs up anger." As you speak, listen closely to your words. Are they gentle or are they harsh?

According to Proverbs 29:11, "A fool gives full vent to his anger, but a wise man keeps himself under control." As you talk to your friend, remain calm!

• Privately confront.—Avoid embarrassing your friend by publicly confronting him or her. No one wants their "dirty laundry" aired in public. There may be a situation where you would feel more comfortable taking someone with you when you confront another person. Be sure the person you are confronting does not feel outnumbered or intimidated.

• Caringly confront.—Your love and concern for your friend must be obvious. Let them know you are talking to them because you care and you want to help.

• Constructively confront.—Avoid the tendency to place blame on the person or to make him or her feel guilty. It's not your responsibility to punish. Their sin will have natural consequences. God will deal with His people in His own time and in His own way. Your motivation for confrontation needs to be to bring healing. As you speak, work to encourage and edify.

• Acceptantly confront.—Obviously, if you are confronting a

person, it is because you believe there is an area of their life that is not meeting the standards God has established for His children. You obviously love this person and care very deeply for him or her or you would not take the time and energy to deal with them. At the same time, the sin needs to be confronted. As you talk with your friend, make sure he or she understands that it is the activity in his or her life you are addressing, not him or her as a person. Even though you do not approve of what this individual is involved in, you still love and accept this person.

• Forgivingly confront.— Many times when people let us down or hurt us, our disappointment in them is overwhelming. Our self-centeredness kicks in. We seek revenge instead of grace and mercy. Our hurt feelings blind us to seeing how the other person may be feeling. Time after time in the New Testament we see examples of Christ at work in the lives of saints who had sinned. In Matthew 6:15 Jesus told us, "If you do not forgive men their sins, your Father will not forgive your sins." Our attitude toward another person directly affects our relationship with God. To harbor unforgiveness is sin. Sin keeps you from having the kind of relationship with God He deeply desires to have with you. Deal with your own attitude before you attempt to help someone else deal with theirs. Be certain you have an attitude of forgiveness.

The apostle Paul was very concerned about some things going on in the churches of Galatia. A group of Jewish Christians, Judiazers, were preaching that salvation is not by faith alone, but also by keeping the Jewish law. In fact, they were preaching that to be a good Christian one had to become a good Jew. Keeping the law and circumcision were the least of the acts necessary for you to be a "real" Christian! Peter, one of the apostles of Christ, was in Galatia at the time. Peter never really took a stand for what he knew in his heart to be truth. In fact, Peter actually compromised his beliefs so he would not offend anyone. Paul, however, was offended! Paul charged that Peter actually went against his Christian beliefs by apparently acting like the Judiazers. He was acting like a hypocrite.

Paul was very much a believer of and teacher of salvation by faith and faith alone. If good works, righteous living, and keeping the law were the things that brought salvation to people, no one would ever be able to experience salvation. No one is good enough to earn his or her own salvation. Salvation was bought with the blood of Christ and that blood is totally sufficient to meet the need. Paul knew that the teaching going on in Galatia was wrong!

Read Galatians 2:1-11. Look closely at verse 11 where Paul said, "When Peter came to Antioch, I opposed him to his face, because he was clearly in the wrong."

Verse 7 tells us Peter was a pillar in the church. Paul knew Peter had gotten off track. Paul knew that he had to talk to Peter before any more damage was done to the church. So, Paul confronted Peter. Think about the way Paul confronted Peter. He did not go to the other pillars of the church and discuss it with them. He did not go on a letter writing campaign encouraging people not to follow Peter. Instead, he confronted Peter face-to-face. They sat down and talked together about the situation.

People make mistakes. Sometimes God uses another person to help clear up misunderstandings and mistakes. If you believe someone is doing harm to themselves or someone else, God may be leading you to be a confronter.

Take a few minutes right now and think about a person in your life for whom you have been concerned. Carefully assess this person's situation? What do you need to be doing to help him or her that you are not currently doing? If you decide you need to confront a friend, ask yourself what is your motivation for doing so. Look back over the guidelines for confrontation. Make sure you are on the right track before you attempt to confront a friend.

Jill Hopson, youth minister at Southland Baptist Church in San Angelo, TX, is the writer of this lesson.

EXTRA CREDIT

1. Look up the words *brother* and *rebuke* in a Concordance and list at least 10 verses that have to do with the proper way to confront a friend.
2. Memorize Luke 17:3.
3. Set up an interview with a person on your church staff to talk to them about confrontational ministry.
4. Before you can confront another, it is important to deal with the sin in your own life. List all the areas in your life where you may need to seek forgiveness from God, a person, or both.
5. Write a prayer to God and a possible reply from God concerning an issue about which you may need to confront a friend.

Service at Any Cost

by Nancy Hamilton

The ring has been bought, the invitations ordered, the prom is soon approaching. You are waiting for probably the biggest day of your life—graduation! As you think about the journey ahead, some of your plans may include college or full-time employment. In whatever journey you decide, you have been called to represent Christ wherever you are, at all times.

The cost of being a true Christ follower demands you to become like Christ in words and in action! As a servant of Christ, you have agreed to meet needs of persons right where you are.

Are you a true disciple of Christ? What have you given up in order to be Christ to someone else in your world? What cost have you paid to be a witness of God where you are?

As a high school student you may have felt you lacked the necessary skills to be a true Christ follower or that only "holy-rollers" are able to share Christ. With God on your side and a willing spirit, you are equipped to reach your friends better than anyone else. As you look to the future—are you ready for the ride of your life?

Ready? Set? Let's Go! What things are you willing to give up to follow Christ? In Matthew 19:16-30, Jesus told a story of a rich young ruler who wanted to be a true follower, yet realized that following Christ had a cost. There are some lessons to learn from this passage.

In order to be a servant, one must be willing to follow Christ. Unfortunately, this rich young ruler was not willing to give up his life to follow Christ at that time. There were other things in this young man's life he held as greater value than Christ. In order to be a true servant, one must follow Christ in every aspect of one's life.

What are some things you follow now that may determine your future?

In being a true servant of Christ, one must follow Christ not only with words, but a lifestyle. There are some persons who feel God wants them to live this lifestyle as a career. Southern Baptists have over 4000 persons who serve as career missionaries. These folks have said, "I am willing to pay the cost to be a Christ follower." Many of these people have left their families, friends, and homes to serve God.

Another aspect of being a servant means you are willing to sacrifice.

Each year, thousands of teenagers are involved in mission projects that help put action to the message they believe through mission programs such as M-Fuge camps, Acteen Activators, Challengers, World-Changers, Sojourners, Elijah Teams, and many other International Mission Board and North American Mission Board and various state mission programs. These students take time out of their schedule to be "on mission" because they want to make a difference in their world. They sacrifice something for the cause of Christ. Some may give up their summer vacations, breaks, family time, or jobs to follow Christ in this way.

What kind of things have you sacrificed and given up to become a true Christ follower?

Some things you could do will require a sacrifice of time, such as:
- Begin a prayer group on your campus at a certain time each week to pray for your peers, your teachers, our country's leadership.
- Spend a few hours a week doing housework or baby-sitting for a single-parent family.
- Serve meals at a homeless shelter.
- Tutor in an after-school program.
- Lead worship at an off-site location, such as a housing project, community center, or public facility, and invite the community.
- Spend your school holidays to begin a church in a newly developed area?
- Do special programs at Nursing Homes or Retirement Centers.
- Conduct Backyard Bible Clubs in neighborhoods around your city.

Other areas of missions require a sacrifice of money, such as:
- Spare a coke a week and give the funds to an offering to assist those who may not have any food.
- Give money to help friends who need financial assistance to go on a mission trip.
- Give to offerings for North American, International, or your state missions.
- Cut back your trips to the movies and give the money left over to World Hunger.

what cost will you share Christ
th others as a servant leader?

- Give up that pair of "Doc Martens" you have been dying to get and buy shoes for some underprivileged kids.

Anything of value has a cost. The reality of the rich young ruler was that he was not willing to do what Christ asked him to do in order to be a disciple. He apparently thought his riches could buy his way into the kingdom. Since he was not willing to pay the cost and make the sacrifice, he went away unfulfilled. The Message translation says Jesus told the man, "If you want to enter the life of God—just do what he tells you." Sometimes we only hear the parts of Jesus' message we want to hear. Hearing Jesus' response was the last thing the young man wanted to hear. He was holding on so tight to his life that he could not give Christ control.

Jesus allowed him to make a choice whether to follow Him—just as He does with you. You are able to determine your future. Now you must count the cost. The return has great rewards—do not hesitate and go unblessed as the ruler did. What is your sacrifice?

Making a Difference. . .

Another urgency of being a true servant of Christ is that your service makes a difference.

Think about your church—what would your town or neighborhood be like if your church was not present in your community? You would have no place to worship, no place to go for spiritual challenge and Christian fellowship. Your church is a key place where you can make a difference. What are your gifts? What do you enjoy doing to help others? Your local church can help equip you to carry the message of Christ to your peers and make a difference in their lives. Are there less fortunate communities around you that need help? Are there health problems that could use your assistance? What kind of social issues are being addressed in your community? Many sociologists believe it only takes 2 percent of a people group to bring about change. You must be willing to take the initiative to be "on mission" wherever you are and believe that God will help you.

Your life as a servant only becomes significant when you give away what you possess to help others. Some of the world's greatest programs, such as True Love Waits, See You At the Pole, and First Priority Campus Clubs have radically changed history and made a difference in the lives of many individuals because of a few student's desire to make a difference. Be a part of that 2 percent!

At the beginning of this article, you were asked what you have given up in order to be Christ to someone else in your world. At what cost will you share Christ with others as a servant leader?

Nancy Hamilton is employed by the Texas Women's Missionary Union as a Youth Associate.

The **Last Word** on **Intimacy**

Does God understand my need for sexual intimacy?

Scripture Passages:
Genesis 2:24-25;
Matthew 19:6b
1 Corinthians
6:15—7:5;
1 Thessalonians
4:3-5;
Hebrews 13:14
Lesson Truth: God has
a plan to fulfill
your need for
sexual intimacy.
Lesson Aim: To lead
you to understand
God's plan for sex
by:
• explaining sexual
intimacy as both
physical and
spiritual
dimensions of life.
• committing to live
a life of sexual
purity.

The Latest Word on Sex?
Premarital sex—normal. Extramarital
sex—the expected. Incest. Child
pornography. Teachers having sex
with students. A culture that seems to
worship sex. Sexual images
everywhere. Marriage devalued.
Divorce repeated. Commitments
broken. Homosexuality rampant.
National leaders embroiled in sex
scandals.

A cable news script from this
Tuesday? Wrong! These conditions
that sound like today describe
situations up to and into the first
century A.D. when Christianity, then a
new spiritual force, began to confront
cultures outside Palestine. It's the way
things were when Paul and other New
Testament writers wrote the Scripture
passages on which this study is based.

Think back through the last week.
Consider things friends or dates have
said to you; recall pictures or ads
you've seen; remember television
shows and commercials; think about
the words to your favorite songs.

In the space below, record some of the sexual messages aimed at you in recent days.

Did any of these messages get to you? Did they make you think about your own sexual needs? First-century Christians also had needs, and they needed to hear God's first (and last) plan for sexual intimacy, the plan revealed long before and recorded in Genesis. That's where this Bible study begins.

God's First (and Last) Word on Sex. . .

Does God understand your need for sexual intimacy? Consider Genesis 2:24-25, and then answer the question for yourself. Go back in your mind for a moment to the garden of Eden. God saw that Adam needed a companion and helper, and He made Eve especially for Adam. Here the Scriptures record God's plan for sexual intimacy, "For this reason a man will leave his father and mother and be united to his wife, and they will become one flesh."

Complete these biblical principles about sexual intimacy from these verses:

1. Marriage is the sexual relationship God sanctions; this relationship has priority over . . .

2. Sexual union implies spiritual. . .

One more thing, "The man and his wife were both naked, and they felt no shame."

Does God understand your need for sex? He invented it, and when you follow His plan for sexual intimacy in marriage, you can find great joy in God's wonderful gift of sexual intimacy. When sin and shame are missing, sex can be much more than just safe.

A long time after Genesis was written, some Jews of Jesus' day were trying to alter God's unchanging plan for sexual joy and lifelong union. Some of them wanted Jesus to agree that it was all right to divorce their wives "for any and every reason" (Matt. 19:3). Instead of agreeing, Jesus quoted Genesis 2:24, and He added something else, "So they are no longer two, but one. Therefore what God has joined together, let man not separate." From Genesis to Jesus, God's plan for sexual intimacy hadn't changed, and it hasn't changed since.

3. Sexual union involves something creative. How can sexual union fulfill God's plan by creating something physical?

By creating something spiritual?

How long should this new creation last, and why?

Summarize God's unchanging plan for sexual union
One _____ and one _____ for _____.

News from the Sexual Scene. . .

Do you like to eavesdrop? Think about God's plan for spiritual and physical intimacy as you listen in on this true conversation overheard a year ago in a hall of a state university; the speakers were two male students, about 20 years old.

Guy 1: Hi! How's this semester going? I haven't seen you since last spring.

Guy 2: Pretty well, thanks. I guess our classes have all been at different times.

Guy 1: Are you still with _____ (girl)? You said that was going really great the last time I saw you.

Guy 2: We're not together now, but it was quite a fling while it lasted. I mean, at first, I thought I was in heaven. Our relationship was all about sex. She wanted it two or three times a day. She hated it whenever we were apart even for a day or two, and I got where I felt I couldn't live without it for more than a few hours.

Guy 1: So what happened? Why'd you break up?

Guy 2: Well, I finally realized our relationship was all about sex; I mean, there wasn't anything else in it. We weren't really friends; we didn't have anything much in common. I began to wonder if she even liked me, and I knew she didn't love me. Finally, I just left; going on seemed kind of empty.

Guy 1: So, are you with anybody now?

Guy 2: Yeah, but you'll laugh if I tell you about it.

Guy 1: No, I won't; I'm really interested.

Guy 2: ____ and I got together about four months ago. She's really beautiful and a serious student. I met

Any version of sex outside of marriage is sexual sin and is contrary to God's plan for intimacy.

her at a lecture. We're always talking about "big" things. I think this might be "It."

Guy 1: So how's the sex?

Guy 2: That's the part that will make you laugh. But, OK, I'll tell you. There isn't any sex. She's into chastity. She says the spiritual and intellectual parts in a relationship should come first, and she's saving sex for marriage. And she expects me to abstain, too. She says if I can't be faithful now, I can't be faithful later.

Guy 1: I'm surprised you're still hanging in there, knowing you.

Guy 2: I'm surprised, too, but, you know, I'm beginning to get more into this relationship than I ever have before. I know things about her; I care about her. She wants us to go to church together, and I'm thinking about it. It's a whole new thing.

Guy 1: Well, wow! I'm shocked. I'd like to hear more, but I guess I'd better go to class. Good luck, and keep me posted.

Sex in the Sanctuary? In the time of Paul, Corinth was a famous Greek city. Paul helped establish the first Christian church there (Acts 18). Greeks worshiped many gods and goddesses, and Corinth was infamous as a place where sexual morals were especially loose. At one time, at the temple of Aphrodite in Corinth as many as 1000 temple prostitutes serviced the "worshipers." Many of the new Christians in the Corinthian church came from this wide-open sexual background.

In 1 Corinthians 6:15-17, Paul used a horrifying image to show the Corinthians (and us) a true picture of the awfulness of sexual sin. Before their conversion, some of the Christian Corinthians may have frequented prostitutes; old habits are hard to break. Paul reminded them that Christians are "members of Christ" (v. 15); that is, we are parts of Christ's body (the church), and He lives in us. Christians' union with Christ is spiritual; we are "one with him in spirit" (v. 17). Paul's reminder (v. 15) is followed by a shocking question, "Shall I then take the members of Christ and unite them with a prostitute?" The thought is abominable, and may not be a bad one to call to mind when you are tempted with sexual sin. Any version of sex outside of marriage is sexual sin and is contrary to God's plan for intimacy.

Probably you find the idea of sexual sin in your church sanctuary appalling, and you should. We honor our church sanctuaries as places

dedicated to God. According to 1 Corinthians 6:19, anytime a Christian sins sexually, he or she sins in a holy temple; "Do you not know that your body is a temple of the Holy Spirit" (v. 19). Once you recognize that you yourself are the sanctuary of God's Holy Spirit and that "you are not your own; you were bought at a price" (vv. 19-20), you must respond in the ways these Scripture verses recommend.

1. Flee _____

_____ _____ .

(We flee from that which hurts us. First Cor. 6:18 states that one who sins sexually hurts himself.)

2. Honor _____

_____ _____ _____ .

Get Ready; Get Set; Don't Go There—Until Your Mind's Made Up. . . Stop for a moment and think back to the garden of Eden and to God's simple and unchanging plan for sexual intimacy. How does Corinth's sexual value system compare to God's? Pretty shocking contrast? Well, catch a hold of this. Soon, you'll claim all the rights of young adulthood. Perhaps you'll leave a Christian home and church for independent life without parents watching what you do. The following are real situations from young adult life in America today. Check those you expect to confront in your new life setting.

_____ **Coed dorms**
_____ **Single-sex dorms with unrestricted visits from the opposite sex**
_____ **A roommate who invites the opposite sex to "visit" overnight**
_____ **Apartment life with no rules**
_____ **Sexually explicit student entertainments**
_____ **Contraception distribution,**

in the health center or on the street

_____ Lewd movies shown for "art" or "literature" learning in classes

_____ Required reading of books that violate your sexual standards

_____ Professors who mock Judeo-Christian sexual standards

_____ College newspaper articles about sexual techniques

_____ Pressure from dates or same-sex peers to participate in sex

_____ Date rape drugs

_____ Rampant binge drinking and connected incidences of illicit sex

_____ Sexually transmitted diseases, including A.I.D.S.

_____ Sexually explicit magazines and Internet pornography

You can't help facing the real world. Your protection is God's Spirit within you.

Paul's advice about sex wasn't all negative. He recognized marriage as God's answer to humans' need for sexual intimacy. In 1 Corinthians 7:1-5, Paul instructed Christian husbands and wives to fulfill each others' sexual needs and to abstain from sex with each other only by mutual agreement, and then only temporarily, if they desired to devote themselves more completely to prayer (v. 5). Husbands and wives, according to Paul, hold ownership in each other's bodies, a pretty radical idea, actually (v. 4).

Circle the word you think summarizes God's message about sex within marriage.

yes   no

Sex and the Sanctified?

In the new life you're quickly approaching, you'll probably hear some "new" views on sex. Who might you hear each of the following from?

"True Love Waits? That's so high school." _____

"Christian standards for sex? Only 10 percent of the population could possibly live that way!"

_____

"Nobody will ever know. Nobody will get hurt." _____

"You must not like girls; I guess you've got a different lifestyle." _____

You are old enough now to make your own decision as a consenting adult. _____

In 1 Thessalonians 4:3-5, Paul had sexual advice for the Thessalonian Christians who lived as a persecuted minority in a very immoral society. He pointed out that God had a purpose in mind for the Thessalonian Christians. He wanted them to be "sanctified," or set apart for His Service. We all like to fit in, and the sometimes scary truth is that Christians are NOT going to fit in a sinful society. We are not like those who know no God, who recognize no spiritual reason to avoid being ruled by "lust" (v. 4). Christians choose to live in sexual purity because we choose to honor God with our lives and because we choose not to do wrong to others (v. 5).

Nobody Will Get Hurt?

If you had sex outside of marriage, how could you hurt
- yourself;
- your partner;
- your partner's spouse, or your own (if married);

ur life
ere on
arth is
emporary,
nd in it
e look
orward to
life with
od in
eaven
hat will
ever end.

- your parents;
- your siblings;
- your roommate;
- your campus and/or church pastor;
- an unborn child;
- your Christian teachers?

Better than Sex? God's plan for sexual and spiritual intimacy is wonderful and fulfilling, and Christian marriage is a great comfort on the long journey we call life. Christian marriage, though, like earthly life, comes to an end when we die. A relationship with a spouse is always secondary to our relationship with God. Our life here on earth is temporary, and in it we look forward to a life with God in heaven that will never end. Believing these things about Christians' eternal future with God in Christ challenges all Christians to live in a special way. As the writer of Hebrews 13:14 put it, "For here we do not have an enduring city, but we are looking for the city that is to come." Any small sacrifice made on earth could never compare to the joy of hearing Jesus say, "Well done, good

TRUE LOVE WAITS GOES CAMPUS

TRUE LOVE WAITS COMMITMENT

Believing that True Love Waits, I make a commitment to God, myself, my family, my friends, my future mate, and my future children to be sexually abstinent from this day until the day I enter a biblical marriage relationship

Signed _____
Dated _____

and faithful servant!" (Matt. 25:21).

This True Love Waits pledge card may look familiar to you. Perhaps you have signed one already. If not, prayerfully consider making this your pledge as you embark on a new phase of life. Even if in the past you have violated God's only plan for sexual intimacy, you can receive His forgiveness and once again live by His plan in this area of your life. Remember, all Christians are forgiven sinners!

Some practical suggestions below may help you fulfill your pledge to wait for sex until you enter into Christian marriage. Check those you can and will do.

____ If you go to college, immediately upon arrival get involved in your Baptist campus ministry group and with the college group at a local church. Here you'll be more likely to meet the people who will share your sexual values and support you in your decision to wait. On a 1996 survey of one thousand randomly-selected Dartmouth College students, the strongest indicator a person would not participate in casual sex was membership in a campus religious organization.

____ Try to live with roommates who also are Christians and who share your values. If this is not possible the first semester, it may be possible after you get to know people.

____ Separate fact from myth. It's not true that "everyone" does it. For instance, on the survey of sexual practices quoted above, more than 50 percent of the responding students reported that they had NOT had sex in the last year; 46 percent reported they were consciously abstaining from sex.

____ Choose your dates from among persons who share your values, and

refuse to continue a relationship that you know will drag you away from your commitment to God's plan for sexual fulfillment in marriage.

____ Pray frequently for the marriage partner God may someday bring into your life. Pray for his or her safety, spiritual growth, and sexual purity. Pray for the children God may give to you. Pray that you will become the kind of person your someday spouse would want you to be. Recognize that whether or not you ever marry, you are worthwhile, for "your body is a temple of the Holy Spirit" (1 Cor. 6:19).

Rhoda Royce, college president's spouse from Anderson, SC, and former youth curriculum editor, is the writer of this lesson.

EXTRA CREDIT

1. Write your own True Love Waits commitment statement, sign it, and post it somewhere prominent to remind you of your commitment.
2. Memorize 1 Corinthians 6:19.
3. Make a list of characteristics you hope will be a part of the person you marry. Begin using this list to pray for your future mate.
4. Make a list of helpful guidelines you can use on dates.
5. Write a poem to your future mate in which you share some important things in your life.

Truth
nd Nothing but the
Truth

What is truth?

Absolutely. . . Is there such a thing as truth? Well, 70 percent of your peers are saying no, at least not anything absolute. They are saying things like: nothing can be known for certain, except what you experience in your own life; there is no longer any black and white issues, everything is gray; today it doesn't really matter what you believe, as long as you believe something; everyone is entitled to his or her own opinion; what is right for me may not be right for everyone. The truth has become relative. Many people are saying there is no objective standard of truth. In other words, there are no certain things that are right for all people, for all times, or for all places.

In the space provided, list some of the things you would consider absolutely true.

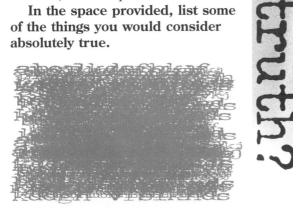

Scripture Passages:
John 3:33; 4:23; 8:32; 10:10; 14:6;1 8:29–38; 2 Timothy 3:14–17; Hebrews 13:8

Lesson Truth: You can place your confidence in the truth of Jesus Christ and His Word.

Lesson Aim: To lead you to experience the truth of Jesus by:
• defining truth in terms of Jesus and the gospel.
• acting on the truth of Jesus by expressing faith in Him.

Let's think about absolute truth for a minute. Red lights. Oh, red may mean stop for you, but I personally like more of a maroon shade for stopping. What about school? Going to school for 12 years in order to graduate (passing each grade, of course)—that may be right for some people, but I think five years is enough for me. Are you getting the picture? Chaos!

Review the list you developed on page 87. Do you think everyone would include these things on their lists as well? Why or why not?

What is truth anyway?— Depending upon how you think, choose one of the following two options (or you could do both! Think of it as a bonus.):

1. Write your best definition for the word *truth*.

2. Draw a picture of truth.

Got 2 B Tru. . . Look up John 3:33 and John 14:6. When I look at these verses, I can define *truth* in one word—God. OK, so maybe you are thinking that is too easy. Let's try to break it down in those terms. If we are going to say God is truth, then we may need to get a firm grasp on exactly what God is like in order to really understand truth. By the end of this session you should understand how knowing some of the characteristics of God can help you understand truth.

If we are going to say God is truth, then we may need to get a firm grasp on exactly what God is like in order to really understand truth.

Try this word-search puzzle. It contains the characteristics of God (truth) we are going to be looking at in this session to help us better understand how to identify the real truth. Look for these words: timeless, redemptive, unwavering, touchable, high-priced, and truth.

```
C T R U N S X I N O Z Q S S I N X
B I U N O Q H T P S I R T C D W S
Z H I T I M E L E S S T H P N X Y
P S B A R E D E M P T I V E H T S
D J L F M U N W A V E R I N G I Z
N Q I V B E T O U C H A B L E J N
T H U D H L F H I G H P R I C E D
A D C I S T H U N O G J L M F I S
B Z H I G H O N J K M I L S S O N
```

Let's use an acrostic to help us look at some of the characteristics of God identified in the word-search above, which should also help us identify truth.

T—timeless
R—redemptive
U—unwavering
T—touchable
H—high-priced

Timeless.—Have you ever felt as if your parents just do not understand you? They were teenagers at one time, but it has been so long they don't remember how it feels to be you. After all, they were teenagers before the Internet and cable TV. There are some things that do remain the same over time. Jesus tells us in John 14:6, "I am the way, the truth, and the life; no one comes to the Father, except through me." Hebrews 13:8 says, "Jesus Christ is the same yesterday and today and forever." If God is the truth and if God is the same yesterday, today, and forever, then would that not suggest truth is also the same yesterday, today,

and forever? Most of you are about to make a big transition into life beyond high school, which is full of change, change, and more change. It would help you to know there is something that does remain the same, no matter if it's the '50s, '80s, or a new millennium. Doesn't that make it easier to think we do not have to redefine the truth every time the calendar changes?

Redemptive.—I am sure that all of you have heard that the truth will set you free. Have you ever told a lie and tried to cover it up for a while? How did you feel when you finally told the truth, whether it be because you had to or you made the decision to tell it on your own? If you are like me, although there are consequences to pay for the lie, they are so much better than keeping the secret. It feels like an incredible weight has been lifted off your shoulders. There is actually a biblical basis for that statement. John 8:32 says, "Then you shall know the truth, and the truth will set you free."

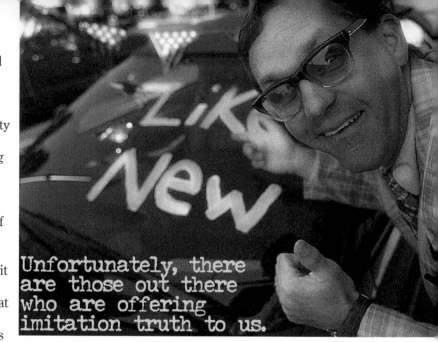

The world often causes us to think Christianity is something that enslaves us—just a long list of do's and don'ts. However, it is actually our sin that traps us. God offers

Unfortunately, there are those out there who are offering imitation truth to us.

us freedom through Christ from our sin. Does that mean we are free to do anything we want? No. It does mean we are free to follow Jesus. Talk about freeing—no matter what you have done, are doing, or ever will do, Jesus loves you now just as much as He did when He died for you. He also wants to have a relationship with you. If Jesus is the truth and the truth will set you free, guess what?—Following Jesus is freedom.

In the space provided, list some things in your life about which you have difficulty telling the truth.

Unwavering.—God does not set a different standard for every person. He desires the same things from all of us. Have you ever wished there were times you could bend the truth or have it not apply to you? It is usually when we are facing a difficult decision or experiencing hard times, that we wish the truth were different for different people. This is one of those traps Satan sets up for us. He wants us to rationalize our choice. However, we need to know God is still there in bad times and during the difficult decisions. God's standard does not change, and the truth still remains the same. We tend to first think that this is a bad thing. However, I think it makes things much easier to realize that I do not have to figure out the truth every time. It is the same for you and me. God loves both of us the same and expects us to maintain the same standard. If we all followed it, think how much easier it would be for us to help each other in those difficult times.

Unfortunately, there are those out there who are offering imitation truth to us. It may seem to work out for a while, but in the end it leads to hurt and destruction. That is what Satan wants to happen. John 10:10 tells us that God is the one who wants to give us the abundant life. Sometimes we get the gift-givers mixed up.

To what kinds of "imitation truth" are you exposed?

Touchable.—God is within our reach. It is really hard for us to understand that the Creator of the universe wants to have a personal relationship with us. But He does! So much so that even when we messed up and created a wall between us and God, He decided to send His Son to restore that relationship with us. He paid the price for our separation so we could be free to know and follow God.

This possibility of a personal relationship is not just for some, but for all. Anyone can have access to the Truth. Do you like to be told the truth? If you are like most of us, of course you do, but yet there are many people who have access to the truth and choose to look over it every day. You are settling for less than the best. Satan sends us many mixed messages disguised as the truth, but it really is just imitation.

Girls, how many of you want to be proposed to and given a cubic zirconia ring instead of diamonds? Guys, how many of you want to make your first million in counterfeit bills? It is easy for us to admit we really want the best—the truth—but when it comes to the most important things in life we settle for imitation.

Max Lucado, in his children's book *Tell Me the Secrets,* uses a great tale entitled, "The Song of the King" to illustrate how the world tries to imitate the truth. Three knights are put to a test to see who will win the hand of the king's daughter. They must make their way through Hemlock forest by following the song the king plays on his flute from the castle wall three times a day. The prince has the only other flute like the king's. The knights are told they can pick one companion to travel with them through the forest. Each of the three knights is known for various characteristics, such as speed, strength, and wisdom. Only one knight, the wisest, made it through the forest successfully. His success was found in his choice of companion—the prince. Since he would encounter many creatures in the forest who would play their false songs on their flutes at the same times the king would play, he knew he would need a companion that could play the song like the king. Traveling closely with the prince allowed him to hear the right tune in order to stay on the right path.

The same principle applies to you and me. If we choose the right companion, the only one who can play the song like the king, we will not be taken off course by the false flutes the world will play as we journey through the forest of life. Jesus is the Way, the Truth, and the Life. Why would we choose any other companion?

High-priced.—Jesus paid a lot for us to have truth and better yet have a relationship with God the Father. He actually paid our debt. In Romans 3:23 we read, "For all have sinned and fall short of the glory of God." Notice the word *all.* This is not just for those really bad people who make the evening news, but for you and me and even those people whom you think have to be perfect. There was only one who was perfect. Yet, He died for you and me. We no longer have to pay that price. In fact, according to Romans 6:23, "For the wages of sin is death, but the gift of God is eternal life in Christ Jesus our Lord." It is our choice where we will live for eternity.

We are given a choice to follow Jesus or not. We are loved unconditionally by someone whom we deny daily by our actions. Talk about a high price to pay. He died for you and me knowing we would continue to sin against God daily. The good news is He loves you right now where you sit and while you are reading. He loves you no matter what you have done or what you will do. You can know that love if you choose to follow Him. He can be your constant source of truth. He can also help you discern truth

from the imitation that surrounds us.

Is the truth sometimes hard to tell? Sometimes it may require paying a price of its own. The times it is hardest to tell the truth is when the price is really high. However, there is no price too high for us when we compare it to the price Jesus paid.

What we also fail to realize at the time is there is a high price to pay for settling for an imitation. Satan certainly makes a good case for imitation. Unfortunately we buy into his imitation trap too often. When we realize we have settled for the imitation, we have to pay consequences for our choice. In a sense we have paid twice as much as if we had just chosen the real thing in the beginning. Standing up for the truth may cost you some things, but if you know the truth and try to hide it, that will cost you much more.

The Truth Will Set You Free. . .

Well, now you understand what I mean by my definition. Truth is God. The characteristics we have noted are just a few of many that can help you answer the question, What is truth? What you have already started doing you can continue to do in the days ahead. Getting to know God and walking with Him daily can help you to discern what the truth is in every situation and how you are to act on it.

If God is truth, it follows that what He says would also be true. Although most of us will probably never experience an audible word from God, we do have a record of His Word for us and how we should live our lives—the Bible.

Read 2 Timothy 3:14-17. According to this passage of Scripture and based on what you have learned about God already, what does it have to do with truth?

What is the value of this recorded truth for us?

If we look at a newspaper, we can see how differently our world defines truth for us. We can see there really is no absolute to them. The truth may not even matter in some cases. After all, what is true for one person definitely doesn't mean it is true for the next. This also reflects how many people see God. A misconception of truth reflects a misconception of God. God really does want to offer you freedom. As John 10:10 says, "The thief comes only to steal, and kill, and destroy; I came that they might have life, and have it to the full." Satan offers many things that are an imitation for the truth and which only lead to destruction. But Jesus came to give us abundant life—freedom. Let the truth set you free and let God's truth in His Word thoroughly equip you for every good work!

Stephanie Wright, youth ministry student at New Orleans Baptist Theological Seminary in New Orleans, LA and assistant to youth ministry professor Alan Jackson, is the writer of this lesson.

EXTRA CREDIT

1. Make a list of all the absolute truths you can think of. Keep the list in your Bible and add to it as you identify more in the future.
2. Memorize John 14:6.
3. Read *Right from Wrong* by Josh McDowell and Bob Hostetler, Word Publishing, 1994.
4. Write a letter to a friend who does not know the truth about Jesus Christ, and share the plan of salvation with him or her.
5. Read the feature "What Should I Do?" on page 94.

What Should I Do?

by Karen Dockrey

You're on your own. No parents. No bedtimes. No curfews. It's both exciting and scary. If you're like most Christians, you know the big dangers—drinking, drugs, sex, crime, and cheating. But there are patterns that cause equally great destruction—time-wasting, sleep-deprivation, short-sightedness, indecision, self-doubt, and hesitation.

How can these cause problems? They're just little things!

Yes, but they contribute to major mistakes. Time-wasting (also procrastination) keeps you from doing well on that fascinating college project. You really wanted to give more time to it, but you and your friends got to talking and you hesitated to cut things off. Before you knew it, eleven o'clock had come and you still had the project to do. Now you're so tired the good ideas you had before won't come. And you don't have time to complete the few ideas that squeak through your sleep-deprived brain.

So you miss the opportunity both to learn and shine.

Well it's just one class. And just one assignment.

Yes, but by not doing your best on this assignment, the professor will miss the marvelous insight and dreams you possess. He will miss inviting you to be on the production team you have dreamed of joining. You also deepen the doubt of making your dreams come true. Because you chose not to decide how long to talk, you squashed a dream.

Yeah, right. All that from a simple night of talking with friends. I thought God wanted us to be people-oriented, not task-oriented.

He wants both. And you can have both with a little decisiveness and planning. Pause the conversation for a a while to get peak hours with which to study. Then talk later. Your choices determine most of what happens in your life. When you are tired, you tend to let someone else decide for you. That will feed indecisiveness, powerlessness, and fear. So it goes.

Spend time studying and then reward yourself with socialization.

How much better will both your social life and study life be if you deliberately choose to balance things—to spend time studying and then reward yourself with socialization, to select classes that both stretch you and fulfill your dreams.

You make decisions sound like some big burden or some big fun-stealer.

Not at all. Deciding to decide gives you fun, gives you friends, and gives you freedom. You find time for study and study becomes more interesting. You involve yourself in ministry and the good spills over into the minutes of each day. You find happiness at work because you work in ways that glorify God. You find time for late-night talks because they're the cap to your week, not the center of your life.

Start by Dreaming

What do you want? Great friends? Good romance? An interesting job? Ways to serve God through everything?

Jot down your dreams and then look at every action as a way to give and receive these. Say, "good idea," during a class discussion to encourage a classmate, which gives him or her the confidence to do well on his test and his future job interview. You serve God in a simple way. And you made a great choice.

But that's a little thing that doesn't make much difference. What about the big choices?

The little choices add up to big choices. They also give you practice so you're primed for the biggies. But how do you make the right choices? T. B. Maston, a huge fan of teenagers, offers these three questions for discovering if a choice is the right one, in his book *Right or Wrong*.

A. How will my participation in this activity affect me?

B. How will it affect others?

C. How will it affect the cause of Jesus Christ?

By working through this simple system of decision making, you will be able to stay true to God's plan for your life while still enjoying relationships and making a difference in them as well.

Continue by Choosing

Scheduling time to be with friends sounds great but what if my friend brings up a big problem right as I'm ready to run to my 12:00 class? I can't just leave her!

Critical to doing the right thing is to decide to decide. Many problems are created just because someone chose not to act.

• Mandy didn't know what to major in. Rather than ask people she trusted, or research fields she might enjoy, Mandy stayed undeclared. This cost her an extra year of college tuition.

• Miller began to lose ground in college math by the second week. Rather than ask for help from the teacher or a fellow student, he just struggled along. His low grade cost him his scholarship.

• Mark knew he and his girlfriend had grown too physical. But it embarrassed him to think about it so he didn't make a choice. Because he didn't want to spoil the romance, he ended up having sex with his girlfriend.

So what about your friend? In addition to T. B. Maston's questions, he also offers three tests for discovering if an action, or lack of action, is right:

1. The test of secrecy—would it be OK if everyone knew it?

2. The test of universality—would it be OK if everyone did it?

3. The test of prayer—can I honestly ask God to come along with me as I do this and bless the action I am doing?

Would you want your professor, parent, scholarship sponsor, or minister to know you skipped class? Would it be good if everyone skipped class to hear a friend's problem? Would you want God to excuse you from class to help a friend? The answers are, no, no, and maybe. So you say to your friend, "Hey, this is serious; let's meet after class for lunch and continue. In the meantime, jot down some possible solutions to the problem. I'll look forward to seeing you in 60 minutes."

You have a choice. Your friend's worry doesn't have to make you miss class. You can choose to leave your friend because you're not leaving her forever; you're just going to class. And yes, you can leave her because someone is already taking care of her—God.

Complete It with Good Counsel

But I'm still afraid I'll hurt my friends' feelings if I tell them to leave while I study or sleep. Aren't we supposed to put people first?

Nobody's born knowing how to do right, be right, or choose right. So get advice from people who know. Ask a senior how he managed to get both studying and socializing done. What did he say when friends wanted to go out instead of hit the books? Or talk to your parents or a professor. They might suggest: "Let's study for a couple of hours, and then we'll reward ourselves with going out for a while." "I really want to talk but I won't be here to talk next year if I fail my classes. So can we meet in your room at 10?" (Then you can leave when you need to rather than push him out of your room.)

Where do you get advice on what to do? Try T.B. Maston's third trio of helpers:

1. The light from within.—God has given you the ability to think, to reason, to judge, to evaluate. You can choose the moral and right thing to do and when to do it. Whether it's a simple decision or a complex one.
2. The light from without.—God has also given you people who are further down the spiritual journey. Because they have faced or watched similar decisions and have had time to see the results, they can advise well. Add their insight to your own.
3. The Light from above.—Jesus has given you Himself, the ultimate knower of present and future. Saturate yourself in the Bible and in daily communication with Him so you can understand what He wants you to do and why.

God has promised you in Psalm 32:8, "I will instruct you and teach you in the way you should go." Let Him show you what to do on everything from who to eat supper with to what vocation to choose. He cares about how you play games, what you talk about, who you grow close to, what you learn, what you worry about, and what you delight in. In every detail you can glorify God or slander Him. Choose the former. Let God use the above questions, tests, and lights to show you just how to spend each of your precious and irreplaceable days.

Karen Dockrey is the author of over 27 books for youth and youth leaders including the Holman Student Bible Dictionary.

The Road to Greatness

How can I attain true greatness?

Who Is the greatest?

Depending on your interest you might answer with the name of an athlete, a movie star, a musician, or a politician. Then again if the question were qualified, your answer may be all together different. Like who is the greatest person who ever lived? who is the greatest person alive? who is the greatest person in your life? Your answers may vary according to the context of the question, your interests, and your life's experiences. I wonder if there is an answer relevant in every context.

Ready for this: Your answer may just reflect your values. What do you value most? Is it something you possess, like a stereo, a car, a CD collection, or memorabilia? Is it an activity, like baseball or band? Do you value things that are intangible, like a friendship or a relationship with a parent?

Start with the Right Question. . .

Whatever it is you value is evidenced in the people you admire. The people you admire and the values you have often determine the direction your life takes. I think it started early when you were first asked, What are you going to be when you grow up? Now you may have been asked this a zillion times, and your answer may have changed each time. The truth is as a soon-to-be high

Scripture Passages:
    Mark 9:33–37;
    10:35–45;
    John 13:3–17;
    Philippians 2:4–8
Lesson Truth: You can attain greatness by serving others.
Lesson Aim: To lead you to seek true greatness by:
    • redefining greatness the way Jesus did.
    • identifying ways you can serve others.

school graduate or a recent graduate, you have already or soon will be making choices that will shape your future. Oh you can still change your mind, but with each choice you make you are determining your life's direction. Whether you are enrolled in college, pursuing a career in the military, or beginning the world of work, the days ahead are filled with opportunity.

Let's go back to the question, What are you going to be when you grow up? You may say, "Who, me, I am never going to grow up." Then again you may be one who decided your career as a child and have been on a direct line to fulfill your dreams ever since. As for me I changed my mind a number of times. In fact, as I reflect on my journey, I was asked the big question a lot. As I graduated and entered college I was clueless. It was almost as if God said, OK, Scott, you don't seem to listen very well, and since you can't see the big picture, I'll lead you step-by-step. My first college major said it all—liberal arts and undecided. I could be almost anything but yet I was still undecided. As my freshman year passed, I soon zeroed in on education and psychology.

As I reflect on my experiences just before graduation and the first years of college, I asked myself the same question. Now, years later, I sometimes look back and wonder if I found the answer. Or maybe it is not the answer to the question, but the question itself. I wonder, what if we were asked a different question as a child, a teenager, and a young adult? How would you respond if you were asked, How do you want to live your life? How do you hope others will describe you? Here is a list. Take a minute and underline those that describe you as others see you?

Blanks are available for you to add your own adjectives.

Giving
Selfish
Greedy
Caring
Self-centered
Friendly
Self-serving
Honest
Hospitable
Uncaring-caring
Sincere
Unfriendly
Insincere

_____

_____

Now review the list again, and this time circle the words you wished described you. I hope you find yourself circling the same words you underlined, if the words are honorable attributes. If they are less than honorable, or even if the underlined and circled words are two different lists, take note. Here's a great place to start if you really want to be great.

Right or Left— How Can I Become a Great Person?
How would you describe someone who is great? **Review the words from the exercise above and list the top five characteristics that define greatness from the world's point of view, according to the Bible, and then from your point of view.**
Consider the subject of greatness, Read Mark 9:33-37 in your Bible. Have you ever considered the implications of the story? Maybe you are like me and you read the story, an historical account, all the while shaking your head and saying to yourself, "How foolish. Couldn't they see that Jesus

Characteristic	World's View	Bible's Viewpoint	Your Viewpoint
___	___	___	___
___	___	___	___
___	___	___	___
___	___	___	___

debating greatness while following Jesus? Would we be embarrassed when confronted about our conversation? Would we believe Jesus was leading us into the realm of worldly power and prestige?

was about so much more than worldly greatness We have the advantage of being able to look back on this story. I wonder how we would have responded had we been one of the first disciples during this time period? Would we be

If You Want to Be First, Be Last. . .

We've defined greatness as the world defines greatness. We've rephrased the question from "What are you going to do when you grow up?" to "How do you want to live your life?" which leads to reflect on what others think of you. Where do the definitions, questions, and reflections bring us?

The answer is in Jesus' response and how He defined His answer day-by-day, action-by-action. Let's look at the story in Capernaum. Mark gave us the account of Jesus asking the disciples about their discussion as they approached the town. Interestingly, the disciples were silent. Maybe more interesting was that Jesus asked, for He knew all things. Even in their silence, He knew their hearts. His words, "If anyone wants to be first, he must be the very last, and the servant of all," must have caught them by surprise. Not only was it a reminder that Jesus knew

and the servant of all,"

be first, he must be the very last,

their every thought, the words were a paradox. How could you be first and last or last and first. Then He took a child and said, "Whoever welcomes one of these little children in my name welcomes me; and whoever welcomes me does not welcome me but the one who sent me." This was without a doubt a surprise. Remember, their culture placed men first. To honor a child was unheard of in their day, especially since there was nothing a child could do to return the honor. Only as a child matured into adulthood did he gain importance.

You may be asking yourself what this has to do with graduation, with college, with becoming a success in the career world. Everything! The question in the beginning of the study, Who is the greatest? is answered in Mark's account. Jesus makes it very clear that the greatest is the one who serves. The greatest is one who places others first—one who is more concerned about serving others than getting served.

Remember our questions, What are you going to be when you grow up? and How do you hope others will describe you? I think in Jesus' words to the disciples we find the key. If you long to be great; if you hope others will describe you as friendly, caring, genuine, dependable, then you must place others first.

Do you value things that are intangible, like friendship or relationship with paren

Serve at All Cost. . .

The point is simple, but the lesson is a difficult one to hear. In a culture that challenges you to be your best, to achieve your goals, to race to the top, rarely will you hear the message, "Serve others, place everyone else before yourself." In fact the opposite seems to be true. You'll more likely hear, "Win at all costs. Do whatever it takes to get ahead. It's a dog-eat-dog world out there. Step on whoever you have to in order get to the top."

Essentials for Life After High School

So, What Would Jesus Do?

How can you make a difference in a world that believes the first shall be first? Begin by serving. Look for ways to place others first.

Take a moment and begin a list of things you can do to place others first.

Things I can do to serve others:
1.

2.

3.

It's often easy when thinking of others to think of friends, people in school, people at work, or people in the community. What about your family? Could your quest for greatness begin at home?

Take a moment and begin a list of things you can do to place your family first.

One thing I can do to serve my family is: _____

A second thing I can do to serve family is: _____

A third thing I can do to serve family is: _____

Let's look at another story in Mark 10:35-45. Take a few minutes and read the passage. James and John said, "Teacher, we want you to do for us whatever we ask." To begin with, I think that's a loaded statement. Oh to be courageous enough to say, "Jesus just give me what I ask for. That's all, nothing more." In His own way, Jesus met them where they were and answered, "What do you want me to do for you?" You remember the rest of the story, one wanted to sit on His right and one on His left. Not only had they the courage to ask, they had missed the whole point of Jesus' mission. They were convinced that when Jesus came into His glory there would be a delegation of roles. To sit on His right and His left carried with the position power and authority, or so thought James and John.

Look at Jesus' response. Not only does He chastise them, He makes it very clear that He came not to be served but to serve. You'd think James and John would have seen this evidenced in Jesus' life. Where had they been? It is so clear to you and me. Before we are quick to judge, maybe we would have been as interested in sitting on Jesus' left or right had we been one of His disciples.

What do you think Jesus meant when He said, "The Son of Man did not come to be served, but to serve"? The statement, What would Jesus do? is popular today. Paul wrote to remind the Philippians of Jesus' example and challenged them to do what Jesus would do. Read Philippians 2:4-8.

As you reflect on the gospels, the pictures of Jesus' life depict service. Take a moment and list some ways Jesus served.

So what does Jesus' example mean to you? Is His example one you can follow?

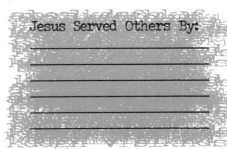

Jesus Served Others By:
_____
_____
_____
_____
_____

According to Jesus, the key to becoming great is to serve. Maybe we could learn from James and John after all. The question they proposed allows us an opportunity to hear Jesus' response. The response is evidenced throughout the Gospels as we view

Jesus' life. Herein is the secret to life that ultimately elicits the response we long for when we consider the question, How do you hope others will describe you?

It's Your Serve. . .

Let's consider another passage. John told about Jesus washing the disciples' feet in chapter 13 of his gospel. Read verses 3-17. Here we find Jesus rebuking Peter. In His words, "You call me Teacher and Lord; and rightly so, for that is what I am. Now that I, your Lord and Teacher have washed your feet, you also should wash one another's feet. I have set you an example that you should do as I have done for you" (John 13:13-15).

This is another clear example of service. The operative phrase, "Now that I, your Lord and Teacher" is key. Evidence of a surrendered life is a life patterned after Christ's example. As a Christian in the career world, in the military, or in college, you will have numerous opportunities to share Christ through your example of service. How many times do we commit to doing great things for God, but when the things don't seem to be so great, we find an excuse; we take an alternate route; we slip out of the room?

List three of the most common excuses you and your friends use for not doing small things for God.

1.

2.

3.

Begin today to serve others and when tomorrow comes, continue to serve.

Jesus' example was perplexing to the disciples and people of His day. Then again, His example is just as perplexing and confusing to people of our day. Remember the list of characteristics you identified earlier. Let's just suppose you chose to do two or three today. How would your friends respond? How would your family respond? Let's take a towel and wash a friend's feet. First, they would likely be reluctant to allow you to touch their feet. And then they would look at you like you were crazy.

OK, maybe washing a friend's feet isn't the best example. To fully understand the nature of Jesus' actions, remember the roads were not paved in Jesus' day, nor did they have sidewalks. As for shoes, most everyone wore sandals. As for transportation, the primary mode of travel was by foot. Remember the days of summer as a child and you had been barefoot for days? When it came to bath time, you were a mess. There was more dirt on you than in the yard. Your feet looked like brown shoes, or a permanent tan. You see, the offer to wash one's feet in Jesus' day, was a true act of service, of placing someone above you. In fact, those of means had servants whose many tasks included washing feet.

The Quest for Greatness Begins Each Day. . .

Look back at your list of ways to place others first on page 100. Do some of these seem despicable—I mean, are they things you could never see yourself doing. If you're going to be great and really make a difference in your world, let's be radical. Here's a suggestion: why not set a goal this week to serve someone each day. Maybe it seems insignificant, but I believe it will have an impact that will not only surprise the one you serve, but also you. I know it's really easy to set a goal for the distant weeks to come, but let' do something now. Why wait any longer?

Make a note of one thing you can do to serve others today; to serve your family today.

Today I can serve others by:

Today I can serve my family by:

Look for opportunities today with friends, with family, even with a stranger. Begin today serve others and when tomorrow comes, continue to

serve. Day by day you will find yourself well on your way to greatness. When you ask yourself how others describe you, the question is already answered by your example.

Celebrate who you are and your unique gifts. Grab a towel and wash someone's feet. Above all, Jesus will be honored and your life will be forever changed as you give your life away following the example of Jesus. Remember, IT'S YOUR SERVE!

Scott Allen, youth minister and National Student Ministry consultant at LifeWay Christian Resources of the Southern Baptist Convention in Nashville, TN, is the writer of this lesson.

EXTRA CREDIT

1. Make a list of all the activities in which you are involved. Be sure to include jobs, school, sports, club, and so forth. Then make a list of possible ways you can be a servant in each area.
2. Memorize Mark 10:43-44.
3. Write down the name of the Greatest Christian you know. List the characteristics of the person that makes him or her great. Circle the characteristics that involve service or ministry.
4. Based on this study, write a poem about greatness.
5. Read the feature "Service at Any Cost" on page 77. Jot down some possible ways God might be calling you to serve and the cost of each.

How do I accomplish what others tell me is impossible?

Hangin Tough

Scripture Passages:
Judges 7:19-22
Jeremiah 32:17,27
Luke 1:37;
Romans 4:19-21
2 Corinthians 12:7-10;
Philippians 4:13;
Lesson Truth: You can accomplish the impossible by depending upon God in your life.
Lesson Aim: To lead you to accomplish the impossible by:
• listing selected promises of God.
• asking for God's power to be demonstrated in your life.

Be All You Can Be. . . You may have seen a cartoon several years ago depicting a young man in the office of a military recruiter. The recruiting poster on the wall of the office emphatically urged "Be all that you can be! Join the Army!" As the young man stood before the recruiter's desk, the recruiter said to him, rather bluntly, "Young man, according to these test scores, you already ARE all that you can be!"

You may not have heard such discouraging words spoken to you, but, then again, perhaps you have! Maybe you have been "put down" about some of your ambitions and dreams. Friends or family may say you lack the skills, talent, or intelligence to accomplish the goals you have set. You may have been equally discouraged by what others do NOT say. When you tell of your plans and dreams, they simply look at you! They may not say anything negative, but they don't say anything positive either!

Take a moment to think of some times when someone told you what you wanted to do was impossible. Perhaps it concerned

your efforts to get into a certain college, get a date with a particular person, win an athletic contest, or change an attitude or behavior. List a few examples below.

What should you do or how should you feel in these situations? One of the awesome things about being a Christian is knowing that whatever is a part of God's great plan for your life is possible through His power working in you. In an earlier session we spent time considering God's will for your life. This study will focus on sticking to the task in order to accomplish what some may tell you is impossible.

The Impossible Dream. . .

Let's begin with a man named Gideon, whose story is found in chapters 6–7 of Judges. If you read chapter 6, you will find an angel of the Lord visiting Gideon as Gideon was doing his daily chores.

The angel told him, "The Lord is with you, mighty warrior . . . Go in the strength you have and save Israel out of Midian's hand" (Judg. 6:12,14). Gideon had several firm objections to the reasonableness of the angel's plan.

Read Judges 6:15-17 to find two excuses Gideon gave the angel. List them below.

1.

2.

Yes, Gideon had his reasons, but God had His plan. God knew Gideon felt inadequate for the task. To make a long story much shorter, Gideon asked for several signs and confirmations of God's plan for him to lead the Israelites in overtaking the Midianites. When he finally understood it truly was God working in his life, he took his 300 men (he started with 32,000 but God told him that was too big a crowd!) and defeated the Midianites. Read Judges 7:19-22. Did Gideon accomplish the impossible? Yes! Did he do it on his own strength and wisdom? No!

Do we try to undertake the impossible tasks in our own lives with our own strength and our own wisdom? Many times, yes! In the space below, write a sentence or two concerning what you can learn about God's power through reading the story of Gideon.

Sometimes You Just Have to Play Hurt. . .

Perhaps you are thinking, *But, that was Gideon. There are some things in my life that make it hard to accomplish great things for God.* You are not the only one with such a dilemma. Stop now and read 2 Corinthians 12:7-10.

Paul wrote about a "thorn in my flesh." A thorn doesn't sound like much, does it? It may not appear to compare with some of the difficulties you have in your own life. Your parents may not be supportive of your efforts to live for Christ. You may have *thorn* you may have a dramatic description of Paul's disability.

We don't know what his problem was. Many think it was a physical limitation or illness, such as epilepsy or extreme vision problems. Others believe Paul referred to his constant persecution by those opposed to the gospel. What matters most, though, is that God chose not to remove it despite Paul's earnest prayers.

In 2 Corinthians 12:7-10, we find several basic facts

Perhaps you feel you were shortchanged in a particular skill or talent you believe is vital to accomplishing your goals.

a physical challenge that prevents your body from doing some things you want to do. Or perhaps you feel you were shortchanged in a particular skill or talent you believe is vital to accomplishing your goals. All of your limitations appear much bigger than the "thorn" mentioned by Paul in this passage. However, those who study the original New Testament Greek tell us the word translated *thorn* was capable also of meaning *stake.* It described the long, pointed stakes placed close together in the ground and hidden in order to impale, or spear, the enemy. It also described the sharp stake on which a victim was impaled as a means of torture. If you use the word *stake* instead of the word

concerning Paul's prayer for the removal of his thorn.

1. He begged God three times for the thorn to be removed.

2. God said no, for He wanted Paul to understand His grace and power as sufficient for any of his weaknesses.

3. Paul learned to rejoice in his difficulties, for he understood God's power showed itself greatest when he himself was weakest.

Read verse 10 again. Paul listed the things in which he would rejoice, for they were the areas in which Christ most dramatically could show His power in Paul's life. Fill in the blanks in Paul's sentence printed below with your own weaknesses or difficulties:

"That is why, for Christ's sake, I

delight in _____ *(list a weakness)*, **in** _____ *(list an insult you've endured)*, **in** _____ *(list a hardship)*, **in** _____ *(list a difficulty)*. **For when I am weak, then I am strong.**

Are you able to read aloud that verse with the words you inserted and mean it? Can you thank God for something in your life you'd much rather He remove?

The Amplified Bible expresses verse 9 and 10 in an even more descriptive and colorful way: *But He said to me, My grace—My favor and loving-kindness and mercy—are enough for you, [that is, sufficient against any danger and to enable you to bear the trouble manfully]; for My strength and power are made perfect—fulfilled and completed and show themselves most effective—in [your] weakness. Therefore, I will all the more gladly glory in my weaknesses and infirmities, that the strength and power of Christ, the Messiah, may rest—yes, may pitch a tent [over] and dwell—upon me! So for the sake of Christ, I am well pleased and take pleasure in infirmities, insults, hardships, persecutions, perplexities and distresses; for when I am weak (in human strength), then am I [truly] strong—able, powerful in divine strength.*

In the passage above, underline the portions you often find the hardest to believe. Circle the words reflecting the attitude you most want to put into practice.

Paul used a word picture to describe what the power of Christ did for him. He saw the power of Christ "pitch a tent" over him and his difficulties! Is there an area in your life over which you want Christ's power to pitch a tent of refuge and protection?

Paul obviously didn't feel let down or disappointed by God's response to his prayers. Instead, he understood God's desire to provide all the strength he needed. He understood God's grace was sufficient for any and all of his needs. His needs and limitations led Him to God. They led him to pray. They led him to depend upon God instead of himself. Are you at the point of understanding your access to God's grace and power? Do you believe His grace is sufficient for all of your weaknesses and difficulties? We must believe God is able to accomplish all things He desires in our lives. He will give us all the strength necessary to reach our goals and realize our dreams—if our goals and dreams are within His plan.

What goal in your life seems impossible? List it in the space below. Ask God to help you know whether or not it is part of His plan for you. Then thank Him for the promise He gives in 2 Corinthians 12:9.

It Can Be Done. . . Are there any impossibilities with God? Examine the Scriptures for an answer to this question.

1. Luke 1:37 states clearly that nothing is impossible with God. The situation here concerned both the birth of Jesus to Mary (a virgin birth) and the birth of John to Elizabeth (who was past the childbearing age). The same truth applies to our "impossible" life situations, also. God is able to do as He wishes.

2. Jeremiah 32:17,27 reminds us of God's greatness in creating the heavens and the earth. Verse 17 states, "Nothing is too hard for you." God Himself came to Jeremiah proclaiming His sovereignty (rule) over all mankind and asking, "Is anything too hard for me?" These verses remind us that the God of all creation can create and transform us as He chooses.

3. In Romans 4:19-21 we are reminded of Abraham's faith in God's promise of descendants to him and his childless wife, Sarah. Abraham was "fully persuaded" God was powerful enough to do all He had promised. God's promise to Abraham seemed far-fetched, just as His promises to us may sometimes seem. But God was fully able to keep His promise to Abraham, just as He is able to keep His promises to us. As we aim for the goals we believe God has given us, we must look with determination and perseverance. Consider the following illustration published in *Leadership,* Fall, 1996.

In 1968, the country of Tanzania selected John Stephen Akhwari to represent it in the Olympics held in Mexico City.

Along the racecourse for the marathon, Akhwari stumbled and fell, severely injuring both his knee and ankle. By 7:00 p.m., a runner from Ethiopia had won the race, and all the other competitors had finished and been cared for. Just a few thousand spectators were left in the huge stadium when a police siren at the gate caught their attention.

Limping through the gate came number 36, Akhwari, leg wrapped in a bloody bandage. Those present began to cheer as the courageous man completed the final lap of the race.

Later, a reporter asked Akhwari the question on everyone's mind, "Why did you continue the race after you were so badly injured?"

He replied. "My country did not send me 7,000 miles to begin a race; they sent me to finish the race."

We must have such an attitude when viewing our dreams and goals. If God gives us a task to complete, we must complete it, using the resources and strength He supplies. Read Hebrews 12:1-3.

Reaching the goals and dreams God gives us is much like running a race. A runner gives great consideration to any unnecessary weight in shoes or clothing. If you watch the Olympic track and field competitions, you know a runner wears only that which is necessary to run the race. We, too, must carry only what will help us in the race toward our goals. We must get rid of anything that gets in our way or entangles us—any sin, any unneeded relationship, anything that pulls our attention away from the goal. Our eyes must be fixed on Jesus. He commissions us to finish the race, not merely start it.

One of the most quoted verses in the Bible is Philippians 4:13: I can do everything through him who gives me strength." This Scripture provides a great promise for the challenges God places in our lives as we live for Him. This is not a "Rambo-like" statement of superhuman strength to do anything we might desire. It is a promise that God supplies strength for tasks He assigns or allows.

In the verse preceding this one, Paul made reference to having learned how to face all things—plenty and hunger, abundance and want. He had learned how to deal with all types of circumstances, for he had faced all types of circumstances: imprisonment, beatings, lashings, shipwrecks, nights on the open sea, sleeplessness,

You may feel you are at the edge of a drop of at least 12,000 feet—and without the ropes used by mountain climbers!

hunger, thirst, nakedness. Paul did not despise material things. He could enjoy them when they came to him. Yet, he could get along without them when he had to. He drew upon the inner resources that were his through his relationship with Christ, finding fulfillment even though his outward circumstances might change daily.

We must accept this great provision of God's strength and sufficiency with a humble attitude, however, for the strength is not ours but His. We must not be deceived into thinking our "success" is solely due to our gifts, talents, or abilities. Consider the bungee jumper. He appears to be sailing in the air, effortlessly flying and free. However, he is anything but free! In reality, he is attached to a support by a strong bungee cord. The jumper

isn't self-sufficient. He is free only because of his dependence upon the cord and the structure to which it is tied. We are much like that bungee jumper. We are self-sufficient only in our Christ-sufficiency.

Reach for the Peak. . .

On May 29, 1953, Edmund Hillary and Tenzing Norgay, a Sherpa tribesman from Nepal, became the first two men to reach the top of Mount Everest and return. Hillary, a New Zealand mountain climber who had once been a beekeeper, reached the 29,028-foot summit after climbing part of the way up Everest in 1951 and 1952. *Life* magazine described the final climb to the summit as a trek "up this jagged and frightening ridge, overhung by great snow cornices above a sheer

Edmund Hillary was last seen "reaching for the top." Could those words be said about us as we seek to reach the goals we believe God has given us to achieve? Are we seen "reaching for the top" striving to complete the task we set out to accomplish? Remember: we serve the God who desires to do "immeasurably more than all we ask or imagine, according to his power that is at work within us" (Eph. 3:20). So, go ahead. Reach for that peak!

Jane Wilson Brinkley, youth worker at North Fort Worth Baptist Church in Fort Worth, TX and experienced youth curriculum writer, is the writer of this lesson.

drop of 12,000 feet."

For years Hillary had longed to carry out his impossible dream. It appeared at one point his effort would fail. As clouds began to fall across the face of the mountain, reporters joined together to send this brief summary of his effort to a world awaiting the outcome of the attempt: "Hillary last seen reaching for the top."

What is your God-given goal that seems impossible? Write it in the space below. You may also want to write it on a slip of paper, listing beside it the Scripture passages we've included in this study. Place this paper in a location where you will see it often.

The pathway toward your goal may appear much like the "jagged and frightening ridge" described by *Life* magazine. You may feel you are at the edge of a drop of at least 12,000 feet—and without the ropes used by mountain climbers! But you must remember God's strength and grace are sufficient. If you are seeking to follow His plan, He will provide everything you need. Never give up!

EXTRA CREDIT

1. Identify and list some possible thorns God has allowed in your life. Next to the difficulties, try to list some ways God is using those to better equip you for service.
2. Memorize Ephesians 3:20-21.
3. List five goals you believe God has called you to attain in the next five years. Pray daily for strength to accomplish them.
4. Set up an interview with someone who is living a victorious life but has had to overcome great adversity. Tape the interview and get them to describe God's presence in the midst of his or her difficulty.
5. Read the feature "CrossSeekers Covenant" on page 111.

rossSeekers
ovenant
by Art Herron

CROSS
SEEKERS

What Are the Issues Here?

I have several friends who are about to graduate from high school. As a friend, I am concerned that they adopt the lifestyle during their young adult years that will help make them successful. They are facing new freedom and opportunity as well as many dangerous roads that may lead them into devastating circumstances. Because you are reading this, you are also probably close to making the same transition into young adulthood. I want you to make the same lifestyle choices to help you be successful. Take a minute to complete this simple quiz. For each question, circle one choice.

Life After High School Quiz

1. Are you interested in being successful after high school? *Yes No*

2. Do you think being a young adult will provide you more freedom? *Yes No*

3. Are fewer restrictions in your lifestyle after high school important? *Yes No*

4. Can the process of getting a university diploma improve your life? *Yes No*

5. Are you choosing a school to attend because of your relationship with God? *Yes No*

6. Is it important to stay in touch with your high school friends after graduation? *Yes No*

7. In the university setting, is it important for your social life to improve? *Yes No*

8. As goals are established in the next few months after high school, is your religious faith important for how you will live your life? *Yes No*

9. Do you feel it's important for you to be a person of integrity after high school? *Yes No*

10. Would you like to be godly in all things you do after high school? *Yes No*

Tally your answers:

_____Yes

_____No

What do you think these answers communicate to you as you leave high school? Jot down some thoughts in the space provided.

I hope that wasn't too hard. There were no right or wrong answers? Simply questions designed to help you identify essential issues important for you after high school.

Choosing a Lifestyle

You will make several major decisions affecting your lifestyle in the next few months. To be successful in making the right choices, a guidebook is helpful. Let me share with you what I shared with my friends about making right essential choices as you determine your lifestyle after high school—a guidebook, if you will! Maybe this can be part of your guidebook!

1. Keep your life focused. What

does God want to accomplish in your life? If you remain focused on God's will for your life, you will choose the right essentials for living.

List three essentials for your lifestyle to remain focused on God's plan for your life.

1.
2.
3.

2. Choose the right kind of friends. No longer will you be with the same people all day in basically the same classes who share the same type lifestyle you are accustomed to in high school. The friends you choose will determine many of the values you will embrace. Circle below the areas where your choice of friends will determine your lifestyle as a young adult.

integrity   sexual thoughts   happiness
drug abuse or not   spiritual growth
unhappiness   ability to love/hate   success
relationship to parents   involvement in
church   understand "fun"

Perhaps you checked each one of the boxes. Yep, the right kind of friends you choose in many ways will determine your lifestyle after high school. This is essential!

3. Make spiritual commitments that will last. CrossSeekers is a spiritual movement on the university. It provides structure to your lifestyle in a world that basically says structure is not needed to be successful. It's built on making a commitment to a covenant. Students across the country are committing to radical Christian living through the CrossSeekers Covenant. It includes these six principles:

1. I will be a person of integrity. (2 Timothy 2:15)
   My attitudes and actions reveal my commitment to live the kind of life Christ modeled for me—to speak the truth in love, to stand firm in my convictions, to be honest and trustworthy.
2. I will pursue consistent spiritual growth. (Colossians 2:6-7)
   The Christian life is a continuing journey, and I am committed to a consistent, personal relationship with Jesus Christ, to faithful study of His word, and to regular corporate spiritual growth through the ministry of the New Testament church.
3. I will speak and live a relevant, authentic, and consistent witness. (1 Peter 3:15)
   I will tell others the story of how Jesus changed my life, and I will seek to live a radically changed life each day. I will share the good news of Jesus Christ with courage and boldness.
4. I will seek opportunities to serve in Christ's name. (Luke 4: 18-19)
   I believe God desires to draw all people into a loving, redeeming relationship with Him. As His disciple, I will give myself to be His hands to reach others in ministry and missions.
5. I will honor my body as the temple of God, dedicated to a lifestyle of purity. (1 Corinthians 6:18-20)
   Following the example of Christ, I will keep my body healthy and strong, avoiding temptations and destructive personal vices. I will honor the gift of life by keeping myself sexually pure and free from addictive drugs.
6. I will be godly in all things, Christlike in all relationships. (Colossians 3:12-14)
   In every relationship and in every situation, I will seek to live as Christ would. I will work to heal brokenness, to value each person as a child of God, to avoid petty quarrels and harsh words, to let go of bitterness and resentment that hinder genuine Christian love.

I pray for my friends about to graduate from high school, that they will discover the essentials for successful living after high school. I hope they will discover the principles of the guidebook for life found in the CrossSeekers Covenant. My hope is the same for you during this time of transition.

Art Herron is a consultant for National Student Ministries of LifeWay Christian Resources of the Southern Baptist Convention.

Essentials for Life After High School